AF584764

EWW GROSS

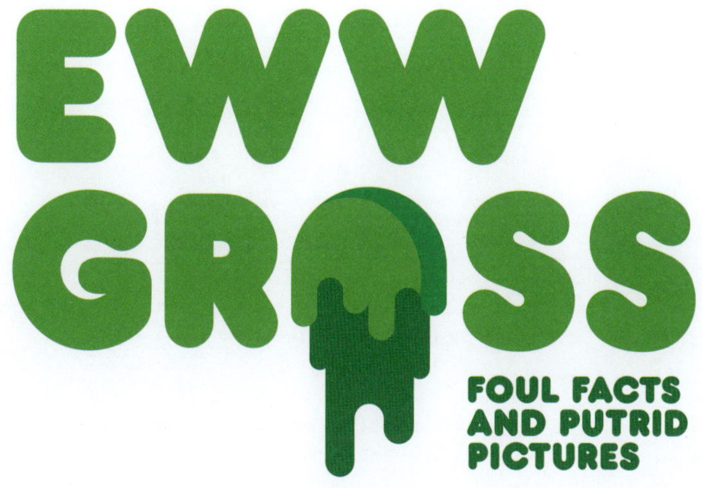

Dan Marshall

LOST THE PLOT

LOST
THE
PLOT

A Lost the Plot book, first published in 2023 by Pantera Press,
an imprint of Hardie Grant Publishing

Pantera Press
Gadigal Country
Level 7, 45 Jones Street
Ultimo NSW 2007

A Cataloguing-in-Publication entry for this book is available from the National Library of Australia.

ISBN 978-0-6456245-6-4 (Hardback)

Cover and internal design: Dan Marshall
Publisher: Martin Green
Editor: Lucy Bell
Proofreader: Farzeen Imtiaz

Printed and bound in China by Shenzhen Jinhao Color Printing Co., Ltd.

Pantera Press policy is to use papers that are natural, renewable and recyclable products made from wood grown in sustainable forests. The logging and manufacturing processes are expected to conform to the environmental regulations of the country of origin.

For Holly, Milly & Winnie.
xx

CONT

ENTS

Hello there, my name is **Slimon**. I love things that are grim, gross, odious, offensive, horrid, horrible, rotten, revolting, despicable and downright disgusting. I also love facts about science. And that's what this book is all about – the filthiest and foulest facts along with the most putrid pictures. You'll also have the chance to do your own gross experiments. You're going to love it, and I'll be right with you all the way to help you learn just how gross our universe is. Let's do this!

Are things gross all on their own, or are they only gross because people think they are?

When you see something disgusting, what happens to your face? What do you feel? Does your stomach turn over, or your throat tighten?

What types of things disgust you? Common things that people find disgusting are: bodily products and insides, such as poo, pee, puke, mucus and boogers; certain foods; things that smell bad; things that are diseased or dying; things that are ugly.

The main facts in this book each get a rating on my **grossometer**. The system goes from **1** to **5**, with only the most revolting facts getting the highest score. But what's gross for one person isn't necessarily gross for another, which is why I want you to rate each fact too. Why not ask your friends what their scores would be? There's a hole in the middle of the grossometer for you to write down what you think the fact should be rated. Maybe you'll agree with me, maybe you won't. There are no right or wrong answers – just as beauty is in the eye of the beholder, so is grossness!

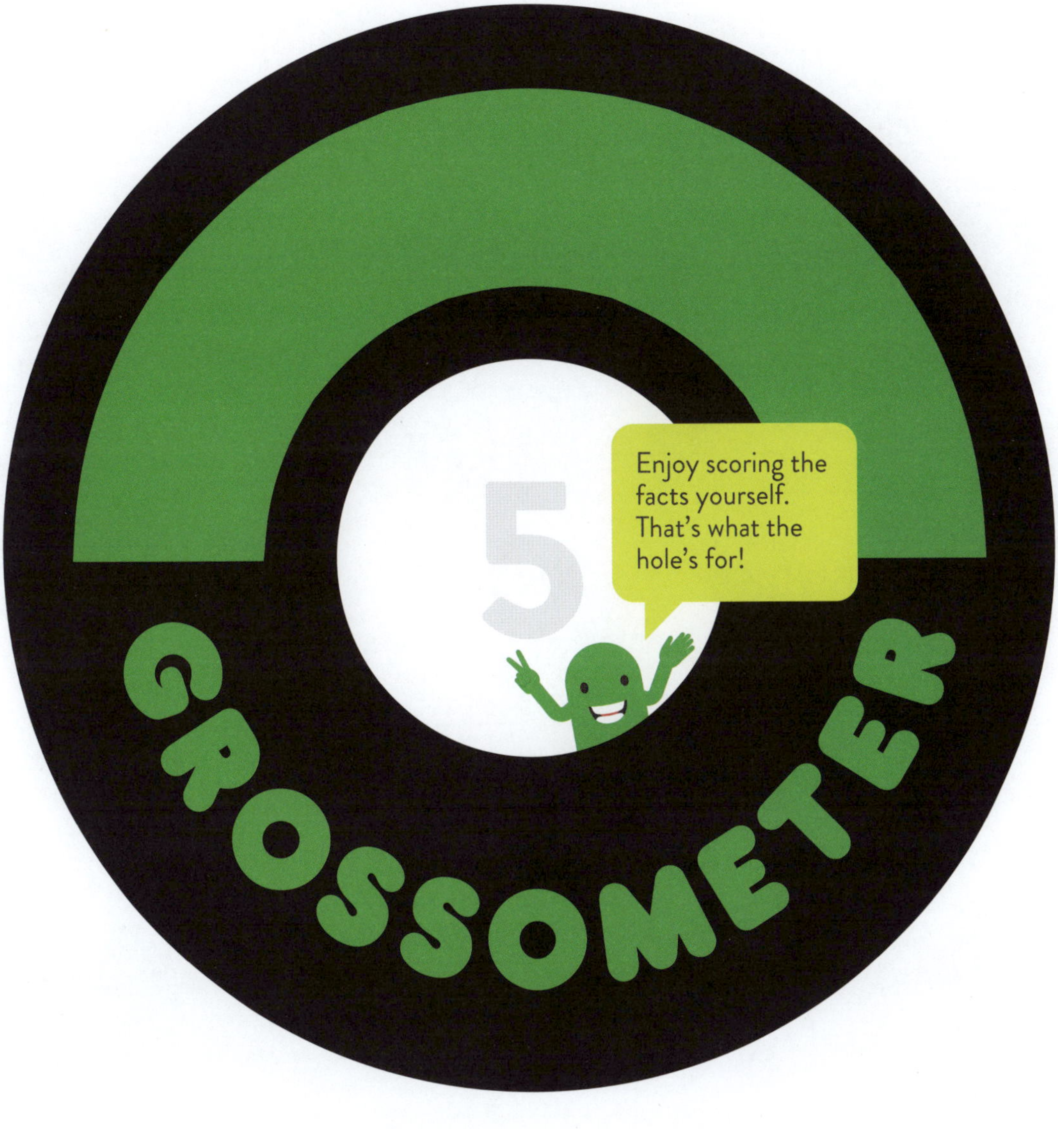

5

Enjoy scoring the facts yourself. That's what the hole's for!

GROSSOMETER

SPA

THERE'S POO ON THE MOON

Littering is something we all try not to do. There's always a bin nearby for us to dispose of our rubbish. But the astronauts on the **6** Apollo moon landing missions did not have this luxury. Because the astronauts aboard those landers collected large amounts of moon rocks to return to Earth, the extra weight had to be offset by leaving some things behind on the moon so the landers could lift off.

This discarded junk included, among other things, **2** golf balls, **12** cameras, **12** pairs of boots, **1** gold-plated telescope and almost **100** bags of human waste. This means that right now there are bags of poo on the surface of the moon. And lots of them!

It isn't just poo that the human waste bags contain. For extra yuckiness, there is also vomit and pee inside them. Eww gross!

Mutant poo

The extreme conditions of the moon's surface wouldn't have allowed any microorganisms in the poo to grow over the past **50** years, but today's astrobiologists are interested in seeing if those microorganisms have undergone any genetic mutations. They're hoping someone will bring the poo back home to study.

Space nappies

During the flight to the moon, the astronauts relied on a plastic bag which was taped to their buttocks to capture poos. A space nappy. It was a revolting and inconvenient process that the astronauts, understandably, did not enjoy.

THE COSMIC STINK BOMB

If our future selves ever manage to leave Earth and explore the depths of outer space, they might encounter a beautiful nebula **5000 light-years** away in the constellation **Puppis**. This is the **Calabash Nebula**, a gas cloud over one quadrillion (**1,000,000,000,000,000**) metres in length.

While it may be beautiful from a distance, up close, things would take a rather pungent turn. The nebula has a lot of the sulphur compounds found in both stink bombs and rotten eggs. For this reason, astronomers have given the nebula the noxious name of the **Rotten Egg Nebula**.

Star Fart

Within the nebula is a red giant star that is undergoing a high energy conversion, a transformation so powerful that the smelly sulphurous molecules are forced out into space. In other words, the nebula is doing a star fart. Cosmic trumps!

Rotten eggs smell so stinky because they produce a toxic gas called **hydrogen sulphide** (H_2S).

This is the incredible speed at which the gas is being forcefully ejected out into space.

OH 231.84 +4.22

This is the technical name for the **Calabash Nebula** – nowhere near as catchy as the **Rotten Egg Nebula**.

The surface of our neighbour Venus is not somewhere you'd want to find yourself. It's hot enough to melt lead and has an atmosphere so thick it would crush you. And, if that wasn't bad enough, it would smell like rotten eggs, thanks to clouds of sulphuric acid.

Our other neighbouring planet is made up of carbon dioxide, sulphur, iron, acids and magnesium. With chemical compounds like that, it's fortunate that we cannot breathe on Mars as the atmosphere too would smell of rotten eggs.

On first impression, Uranus has no smell at all, with an atmosphere consisting mainly of odourless gasses hydrogen and helium. But travel deeper into the planet and thanks to liquid ammonia, hydrogen sulphide, methane and carbon dioxide, you will smell farts.

VENUS

MARS

URANUS

PLANETAR

If you stand in the great outdoors here on Earth and take a really deep breath, chances are you'll smell nothing but clean fresh air. Unless of course you're standing near a particularly smelly farmyard or the elephant enclosure at your local zoo. But this is not the case on other planets in the solar system. Even though humans have not yet set foot on any of these planets, thanks to techniques such as **spectroscopy**,

PONGS

astronomers' telescopes can analyse the light from planets in space. From this, they can figure out what planets are made of – and what they smell of. In other words, we're using our telescopes as noses, taking a huge cosmic sniff, and what we're smelling from some planets is pretty pongy indeed.

Perhaps the smelliest of all the planets in our solar system is the gas giant Jupiter. Its size means that it has different smells depending on what layer of the planet you're at. At the outer layer, the pong you can smell is ammonia, which smells like urine and cleaning products. Travel deeper and you'll smell rotten eggs mixed with ammonia. Double trouble. The heavier layer smells of urine too, but this is mixed with hydrogen cyanide, which smells like bitter almonds or marzipan.

JUPITER

ASTRONAUTS DRINK THEIR OWN PEE

Astronauts aboard the International Space Station (ISS) are fond of the saying, 'Today's coffee is tomorrow's coffee!' which is a polite way of saying that they drink their own recycled urine.

Water is extremely heavy and difficult to transport into orbit, which is why the ISS has to be remarkably resourceful when it comes to recycling. Or should that be 'peecycling'?

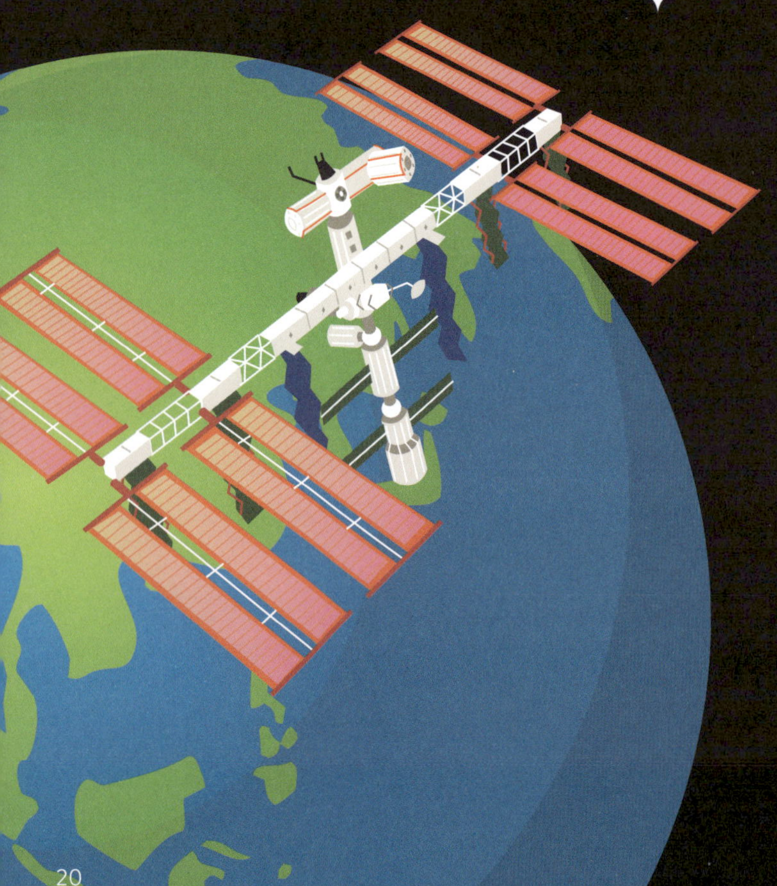

Sweat it out

A special filter takes not only the astronauts' urine, but also their sweat, and over **8 days** the bodily fluids are turned from waste into drinking water. This may sound disgusting, but this water is purer than the water most of us drink from our taps at home. Nice!

730

This is the number of litres of sweat and urine that an astronaut must drink per year to survive aboard the ISS.

Peed off

The ISS has **2** water filtration systems aboard – one that the Americans use and one that the Russians use. The Russian system only recycles their sweat and condensate from the air. They refuse to drink recycled urine, leaving that to their American comrades.

Dirty laundry

So they don't contaminate the water with chemical detergents and make it hard to filter and re-use, astronauts don't wash their clothes. Instead, they wear them until they are too soiled or smelly to deal with. Even their underwear!

DIRTY UNDIES AND TOILET PAPER ARE USED TO GROW PLANTS IN SPACE

The fact that the astronauts on the International Space Station (ISS) don't wash their clothes or underwear led science officer **Don Pettit** to get inventive when it came to growing plants onboard the ship. Since there was no soil, he looked to his dirty undies as a planter solution. He folded his old underwear into a sphere and held it in place with a few stitches. For the outside of the planter, he sewed Russian space toilet paper to the surface. Very clever and very gross.

Growing up

Although old-underwear toilet-paper planters may sound revolting, there are actually nutrients in dirty undies that help plants grow in space.

2

This is the number of days it took for the seeds to sprout in the underwear planter.

DEAD SKIN CLOUDS IN SPACE

GROSSOMETER

Pulling your socks off at the end of the day isn't exactly a gross experience. You pop them off and put them in the linen basket. Easy peasy. But for the astronauts aboard the ISS it's a much more disgusting task. Here on Earth our skin cells molt, and gravity pulls them away from our bodies. However, in space, there's no gravity to pull them away, so the dead skin cells just float. Everywhere. The astronauts are surrounded by clouds of dead skin.

Falling off

Any callouses on the bottom of your feet fall off within **2** to **3** months of living on the ISS.

Suck it up

It isn't just feet that shed skin into the cabin of the ISS; it's your whole body! To prevent huge clouds of skin dust, the astronauts make sure they take their clothes off close to vents that suck up the dead skin cells.

Down the toilet

Aboard the ISS, the same problem applies to clipping nails, shaving and even going to the toilet. Everything needs vacuuming. In 2018, NASA spent **US$23 million** on a new and improved vacuum toilet because the old one needed replacing and was difficult to keep clean. Disgusting!

THE ISS IS MOULDY

One of the challenges of living on the International Space Station (ISS) is that mould grows inside it. And outside it too. The astronauts spend hours each week cleaning the walls to keep mould at bay and prevent them breathing it in and developing infections or more serious lung diseases.

Born survivor

The ISS mould survives **200** times the radiation dose that would kill a human.

Hard to kill

As well as being more resistant to cosmic radiation, the mould spores can withstand extreme temperatures, ultraviolet light, chemicals and dry conditions. This mould is incredibly hard to kill.

LET'S DO THIS!

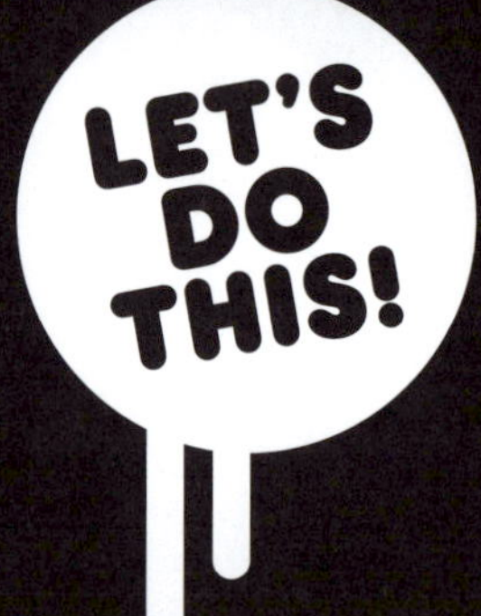

GROWING MOULD

Here on Earth, you can easily set up your own experiment to observe just how fast mould can grow in the right conditions.

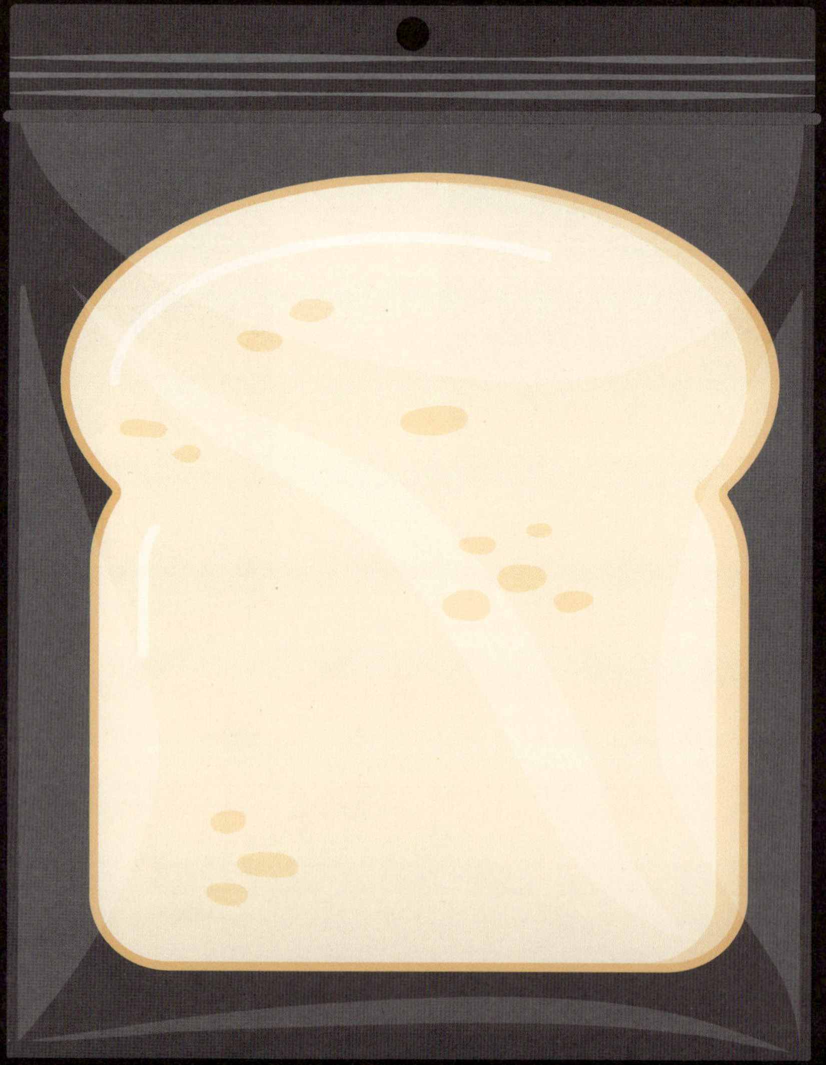

What you will need

Plastic zip lock bag

Bread slice

Water sprayer

How to make the mould

1. Spray some patches of the bread with water
2. Seal the bread inside the plastic bag.
3. Store the bag in a warm area.
4. Observe the mould growth over time.
5. When finished, dispose of the bag carefully without opening it. Wash your hands thoroughly every time you have touched the bag.

It should take around **7–10** days before you see any significant growth on the bread.

SPACE MAKES YOU SICK

GROSSOMETER

Astronauts undergo a lot of anti-gravity training before they travel into space. But no matter how much they prepare, there's no avoiding the fact that for some of them their first few days in space will involve fighting the urge to puke. These poor individuals often come down with 'space sickness' or **Space Adaptation Syndrome** (**SAS**). It's likely caused by a change in gravity and its symptoms include headaches, vertigo, nausea and, in extreme cases, prolonged bouts of vomiting.

Repeat offender

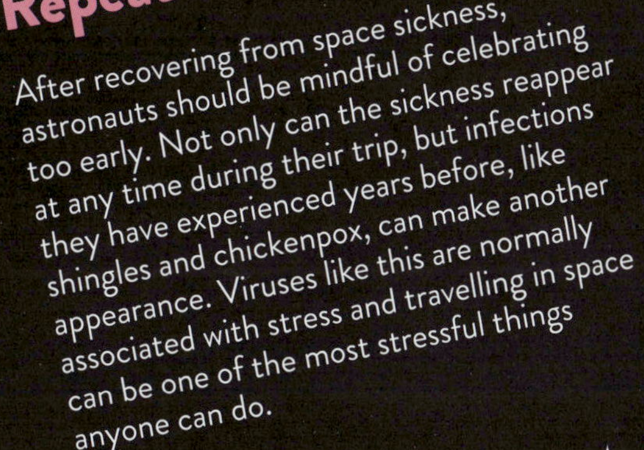

After recovering from space sickness, astronauts should be mindful of celebrating too early. Not only can the sickness reappear at any time during their trip, but infections they have experienced years before, like shingles and chickenpox, can make another appearance. Viruses like this are normally associated with stress and travelling in space can be one of the most stressful things anyone can do.

Sick to death

Astronauts chucking up into their helmets might sound funny, but the reality is far from it. It's incredibly dangerous, especially if they are outside the ship on a spacewalk. Any vomit on the inside of their helmet could effectively blind them. And because their helmets can't be removed, the vomit might be inhaled or clog the astronaut's life support system. Terrifying!

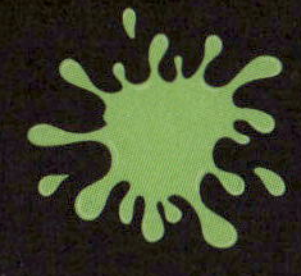

COMETS DO EPIC FARTS

Imagine travelling through space for over ten years and when you finally reach your destination, it smells like eggy horse poo. Well, that's exactly what happened to the **Rosetta**, a space probe launched in 2004, when in 2014 it finally arrived at a comet named **67P/Churyumov-Gerasimenk**. And a very smelly comet it was too – a combination of hydrogen sulphide, ammonia and the suffocating stench of formaldehyde. To make an already pungent situation worse, the comet was emitting huge gassy farts.

Dirty snowball

The comet 67P/Churyumov-Gerasimenk is basically a dirty snowball, made of ice, carbon dioxide, dust and organic molecules. As its orbit brought it nearer to the sun, the ice melted rapidly and boiled off into gas – and it let out a really big comet fart!

Powerful pump

The European Space Agency described the comet's fart as being so dramatic and powerful that it even pushed away the incoming solar wind. That's some pump!

10 METRES PER SECOND

The speed of the fart from **Comet 67P** according to the **Rosetta** space probe. That's over three times as fast as a human breaking wind.

YOUR BLOOD CAN RUN BACKWARDS IN SPACE

Of all the gross things that can happen to astronauts in space, their blood starting to flow backwards is perhaps the yuckiest of all. And it's dangerous too. The lack of gravity causes strange things to happen to some astronauts' bodies and their blood circulation can stall or even completely change direction.

When astronauts return to Earth, this super strange condition disappears completely.

Brain drain

We have a special vein called the **left internal jugular** that moves blood out of our heads when we're lying down. When we stand up, it collapses to prevent too much blood draining out of our noggins. Some astronauts have experienced stalled or even reversed blood flow in this jugular vein, putting them at risk of a blood clot.

Puffy head bird legs

A lack of gravity causes blood to redistribute in astronauts' bodies. When astronauts first arrive in space, the blood vessels in their necks expand due to blood moving to the upper parts of their bodies. This causes their necks and faces to swell and their legs get thinner. They nickname this 'puffy head bird legs'.

Jiggle it

Backwards blood flow in space may be because the lack of gravity causes the organs in an astronaut's chests to jiggle around, pressing on the veins lower down.

IF ALIENS EXIST, THEY WILL LOOK AND SMELL REVOLTING

Nobody knows for sure if there's life out there in the universe, but we do have lots of ideas about what it might be like. It's fun to imagine what wild and wonderful creatures there could be. Little green aliens with big heads, huge dark eyes, two arms and two legs are what a lot of people imagine. In reality though, any alien life probably looks closer to our sea creatures back here on Earth: the really freaky disgusting ones that live in the dark depths of the oceans.

GROSSOMETER

Hot stuff

Wherever we've looked on Earth and found liquid water, we've found life. And there are watery moons in our solar system and beyond that may have exactly the same. On Earth, the erupting hydrothermal seafloor vents are thought to be similar to distant cosmic ocean worlds, including the ice-covered moons **Europa** and **Enceladus**.

Creature feature

The deep superheated seawater on Earth is rich in minerals and provides the heat and energy required for some creatures to thrive in these cold and dark depths, creating a marine park of monstrous tube worms, foot-long clams, blind shrimp and extreme microbes. So just imagine what is happening under the surface on other planets!

Swamp gas

Scientists believe that aliens might not even be oxygen-based life forms like us and could survive on a different gas entirely. One idea is that phosphine, found in marshlands and swamps, could sustain extraterrestrials. Meeting one of these would be a foul-smelling experience as phosphine stinks of garlic or decaying fish.

GROSSOMETER

BLACK HOLES TURN YOU INTO SPAGHETTI

Black holes are powerful beasts. They are areas of space where gravity is so strong that nothing can escape its cosmic pull, not even light. If you ever happened to get close to one of these monsters, the gravity your feet experienced would be much stronger than the gravity acting on your head. Consequently, your feet would start to speed up at a faster rate than your head, and your body would begin to get stretched. Astrophysicists call this **spaghettification** because the incredibly strong gravitational force would pull you into a long, thin piece of spaghetti. Mamma mia!

Snap to it

Spaghettification has a painful and very gross conclusion. You'd snap apart at your weakest point, likely around your midriff, and you might even see your long thin legs floating next to you as they continued to stretch away. Your upper body would go through the same process until each of your body parts snapped for a second time. Before you knew it, you'd no longer be an astronaut, but a group of disconnected atoms vanishing down the black hole.

Rip it up

Spaghettification of astronauts is purely hypothetical and not something that's been proven or even observed. But, using a combination of radio and infrared telescopes, we have witnessed a black hole **20 million times** more massive than the Sun ripping apart a nearby star.

1

SECOND

The time taken for an astronaut to die from **spaghettification.**

As well as spaghettification, astrophysicists sometimes refer to the phenomenon as **the noodle effect**.

THE FIRST EVER SPACE BABIES WERE COCKROACHES

In **2007**, Russian scientists launched into space a unique cosmic traveler – a very small one with six legs and her own antennae. She was a cockroach named Hope and she became the first ever creature to conceive and give birth in space, onboard the unmanned Foton-M bio-satellite.

Shell shock

The scientists noted that the cockroaches born in space matured faster than those born on Earth as their upper shell darkened in colour much earlier compared to Earth-bound cockroaches, who darken up later in their life cycle.

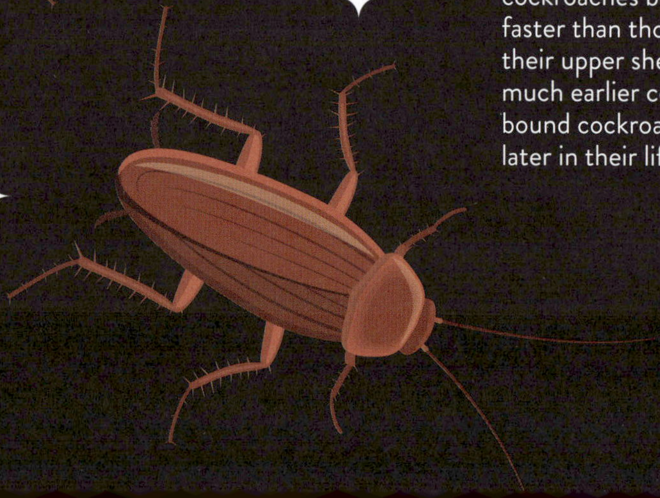

33
This is the number of baby cockroaches who were born onboard the Foton-M bio-satellite.
In **1947**, fruit flies were the first ever insects to be sent into space.
GROSSOMETER

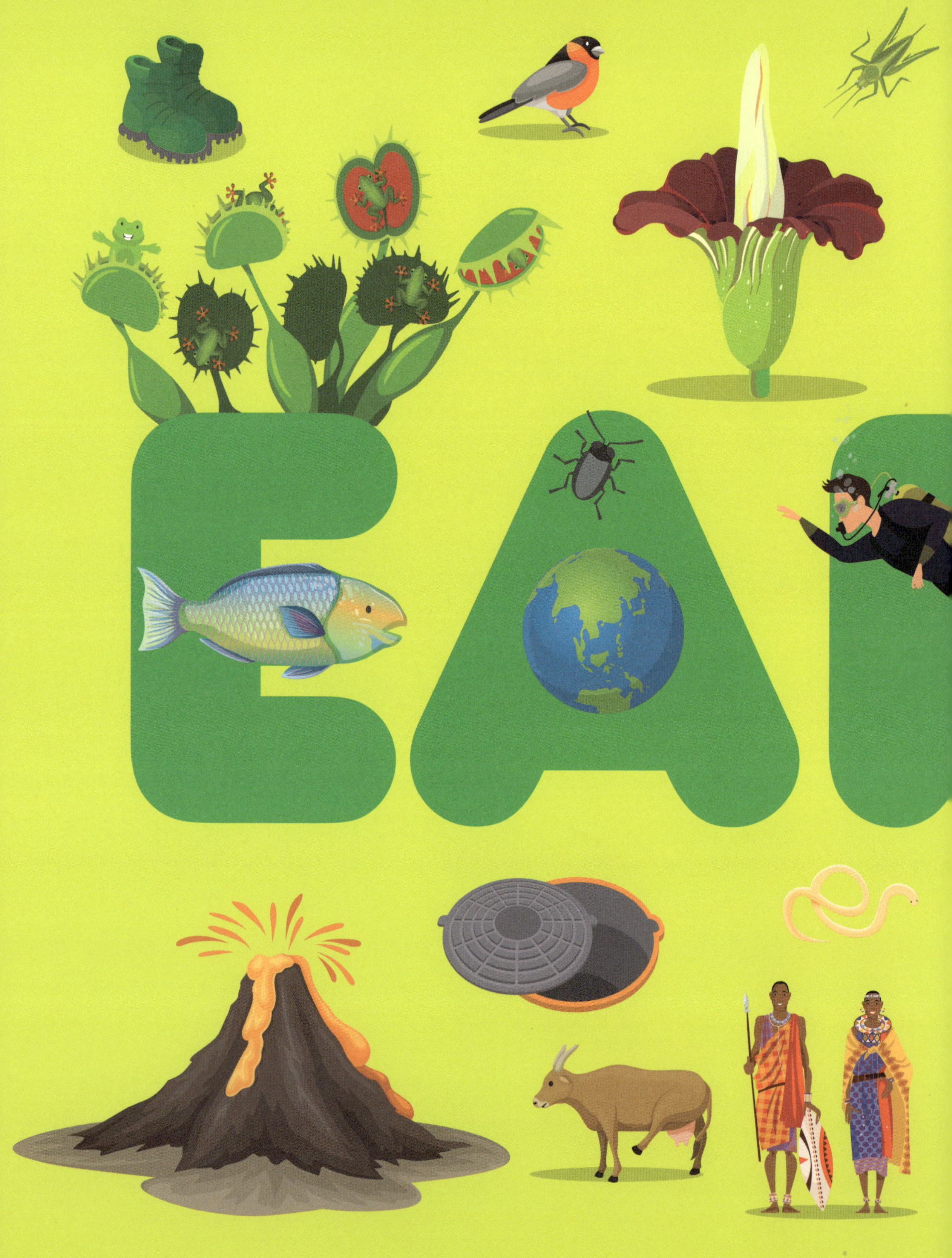
EA

POO

GIANT CORPSE FLOWERS SMELL OF DECOMPOSING MEAT

Flowers are usually associated with the nicer things in life. They're a great gift to brighten up anybody's day, but some flowers you definitely wouldn't want to give to anyone – except maybe your worst enemy. One such flower is referred to as the 'corpse flower' and its stench has been likened to rotting flesh and even to death itself. The smell is so revolting that few people can last long around it. The most famous of these flowers are *Rafflesia arnoldii* and *Amorphophallus titanum*. Hold your nose!

Rafflesia arnoldii

7

The number of days the ***Rafflesia arnoldii*** flower stays open for.

Rotten luck

The corpse flower's satanic scent is a chemical combination that mimics decomposition to attract insects who will help pollinate it. Beetles and flies who are drawn to the smell of decaying meat cannot help themselves and gravitate towards the flowers.

Gentle giants

Both the ***Rafflesia arnoldii*** and the ***Amorphophallus titanum*** are enormous. The former can have a diameter up **1 metre** and the latter can be up to **3 metres** tall. They are giants of the flower world.

Amorphophallus titanum

36

The number of hours the flower stays open for.

10

The number of years for ***Amorphophallus titanum*** to bloom.

Leaf it out

Although massive, the flowering ***Rafflesia arnoldii*** cannot support themselves. They have no leaves, stalks or even roots. They are parasites who rely on their jungle vine hosts for survival.

Getting warmer

Not only does ***Amorphophallus titanum*** fool insects with its smell, but it deceives them further by heating up to **36.7 degrees Celsius** to mimic a dying animal. So clever and so gross.

PLANTS CAN EAT FROGS

When it comes to **Venus flytraps**, the clue to what these peckish plants eat is in the title. Unfortunate flies are lured to the red lining of its leaves, attracted by the fragrant nectar the plant secretes. Once the plant has its prey, it snaps its jaws shut in under a second and begins to digest its fly dinner. But that's not the only thing Venus flytraps like to dine on – these meat-eating beasts like to eat frogs too!

12

The number of days it can take a Venus flytrap to fully digest its food.

Food for thought

Contrary to its name, the main food for Venus flytraps is actually ants. As well as ants, flies and frogs, they also consume crickets, beetles, grasshoppers, spiders, slugs, worms and even little birds!

Spit it out

There are parts of the animals and insects the Venus flytrap captures that it cannot eat, such as the bones and exoskeletons. To deal with this, it simply opens its trap and any undigested parts fall out.

The mechanism that Venus flytraps use to trap their prey is one of the most complex in the entire plant kingdom.

In **Portugal** it is illegal to pee in the ocean.

A LOT OF PEOPLE PEE IN THE OCEAN

Many do it, but few actually admit to doing the dirty deed. Having a cheeky pee in the ocean is something that a lot of people have done at least once in their life – and some more often than others it seems.

Closed for business

One of Thailand's most famous beaches, **Maya Bay**, was closed for over three years due to the large number of tourists peeing in the ocean.

62%

The percentage of people, who when asked, admitted to having peed in the ocean.

974 LITRES

This is the amount of pee a whale does in the ocean every day.

48%

The percentage of people, who when asked, admitted to having peed in the ocean more than once.

POO IS USED TO BUILD HOMES

Living in a home built out of poo might seem revolting at first. It's definitely not the first thing you think of when it comes to building materials to use for your place of residence. However, people have been building with **cow dung** for thousands of years. It's an excellent thermal insulator and features in homes all over the planet. It's environmentally sustainable too. Gross, but good.

As a housing material, poo not only **repels mosquitos** and acts like a **thermal insulator** but it forms a **stable foundation** against natural disasters and is an excellent natural disinfectant. It's also a **serotonin-increasing** mood booster too.

Wax on

In Southern India, cow dung is often used to **wax** the floor. The dung floor, along with the beautiful **Kolam drawings** reminds the inhabitants of their harmonious co-existence with the environment.

Keep your cool

In the Great Rift Valley of Southern Kenya and Northern Tanzania, the **Maasai** people's homes are made of mud, sticks, grass, cow dung and cow pee. This foul fusion keeps mosquitos away and keeps the dwellers cool.

THE MONSTROUS FATBERG UNDER LONDON

In **2018,** a giant monster was discovered in the sewers beneath east London. But this wasn't some hairy subterranean savage, waiting to grab you if you peeked under a manhole. Rather, this was a floating, slimy, monstrous mass of congealed fat that had collected there from years and years of the world above failing to properly deal with their waste. The result was a super-gross **fatberg**.

Stick with it

Fatbergs are normally caused by wet wipes, nappies or other non-biodegradable objects that have been flushed away. Fat and grease, which is incorrectly poured down the sink after cooking, will stick to these objects.

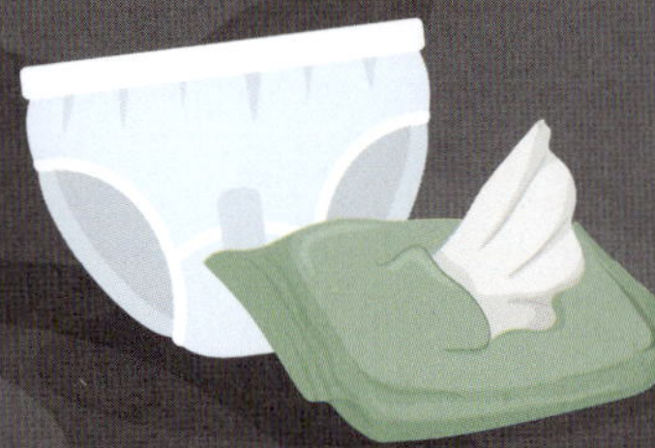

Blockages

Enormous blockages are created as more and more fat and grease sticks to non-biodegradable objects. The sewer system is designed to deal with biodegradable human waste, not kitchen fat, and the fatbergs can cause sewer waste to flood back above ground.

130,000 KILOGRAMS

The estimated weight of the east London fatberg.

The same weight as

19

African elephants.

250 METRES

The length of the east London fatberg.

The same weight as

11

Double decker buses.

244 metres
The length of **Tower Bridge**, London.

The same weight as

2

Airbus A318 aircrafts.

NORTH PACIFIC OCEAN

Subtropical Conergence Zone

Western Garbage Patch

The Grand Pacific Garbage Patch covers an area **3** times the size of France.

Almost **half** of the garbage is made up of discarded fishing gear.

1.8 TRILLION

The estimated number plastic pieces in the Grand Pacific Garbage Patch.

Eastern Garbage Patch

THE TRASH VORTEX IN THE OCEAN THAT'S TOO BIG TO MEASURE

The **Great Pacific Garbage Patch** is a collection of marine debris in the North Pacific Ocean. Circulating currents have created three areas of debris. However, these areas are not giant islands of trash, they consist mainly of tiny plastic bits known as microplastics and cannot always be seen by the naked eye. Rather, the microplastics make the water look like a cloudy soup. Mixing in this soup are larger items like bottles, shoes and fishing gear, which can damage property and entangle, injure, or even drown marine wildlife. Not all the ocean trash floats on the surface. Heavier debris sinks beneath the surface, making the Great Pacific Garbage Patch impossible to measure.

H S H

VOLCANOS SMELL OF ROTTEN EGGS

An erupting volcano is a spectacular sight. The Earth's surface opens, allowing gas, hot lava and ash to escape from beneath the Earth's crust in a breathtaking and fabulous fashion. But if you were actually present at the volcano, it wouldn't just be a visual bombardment; your nose would be twitching too. And not in a good way. That's because the air around you would smell of the most rancid **rotten eggs** – a noxious smell so revolting you'd want to get out of there as fast as you possibly could.

Burning up

The reason for the rotten egg smell around volcanos is **hydrogen sulphide** (H_2S). Although low in toxicity to people, ingesting too much sulphur can cause a burning sensation or diarrhea. The dust you breathe in can irritate your airways and cause coughing, and your skin and eyes would be irritated too. You might even get blurred vision from the stench. Talk about a smell so bad it makes your eyes water!

Mud slinging

As well as volcanos that erupt molten lava, there are also ones that spew out mud. The mud isn't the same staggering temperature as lava – in fact, it's cold to the touch! But it still reeks of rotten eggs. Cold, weird, eggy mud.

Odoriferous eruption

When Iceland's **Bárðarbunga** volcano erupted in **2014**, the smell of rotten eggs could be whiffed as far away as Finland. That's over **2000** kilometres away.

MAKING A VOLCANO

Seeing an erupting volcano up close is a difficult and dangerous task. Here's a way to see a volcanic eruption without the rotten egg smell and running the risk of being burned to a smoldering crisp. And it can be created using items you probably have at home. This experiment involves mixing baking soda and white vinegar to simulate an eruption, and a little bit of modelling using Play-Doh. Since the Play-Doh gets wet, it's a good idea to use old Play-Doh that's starting to dry out a little. You can use a combination of different colours from past play sessions. Happy building!

What you will need

Glass jar

Large plate

1 tablespoon baking soda (sodium bicarbonate)

Food colouring (optional)

Play-Doh

125 millilitres white vinegar

How to make the volcano

1 Place the glass jar on the plate.

2 Add the baking soda to the glass jar. You can also add some food colouring if you want to.

3 Build up Play-Doh around the glass jar and plate to create a volcano shape with a hole around the top of the glass jar.

4 Slowly pour the white vinegar into the volcano.

5 Enjoy the brilliant bubbly eruption!

The vinegar and baking soda react together to create **carbon dioxide** (CO_2) and this gas makes the eruption!

REVOLTING

Museums are not only for displaying dinosaur skeletons and Egyptian artifacts. There are many museums around the world that focus on the grosser side of history and life.

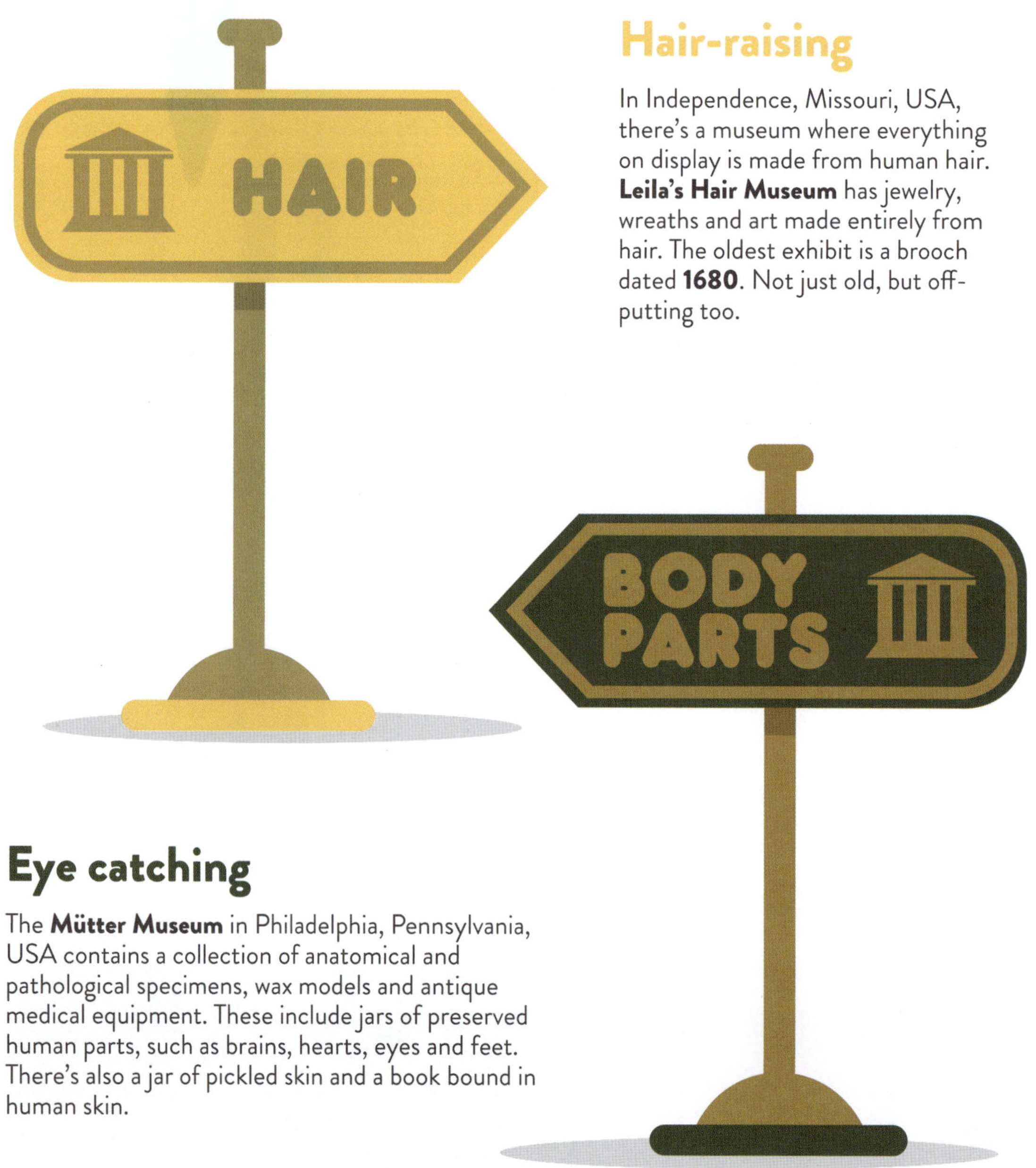

Hair-raising

In Independence, Missouri, USA, there's a museum where everything on display is made from human hair. **Leila's Hair Museum** has jewelry, wreaths and art made entirely from hair. The oldest exhibit is a brooch dated **1680**. Not just old, but off-putting too.

Eye catching

The **Mütter Museum** in Philadelphia, Pennsylvania, USA contains a collection of anatomical and pathological specimens, wax models and antique medical equipment. These include jars of preserved human parts, such as brains, hearts, eyes and feet. There's also a jar of pickled skin and a book bound in human skin.

MUSEUMS

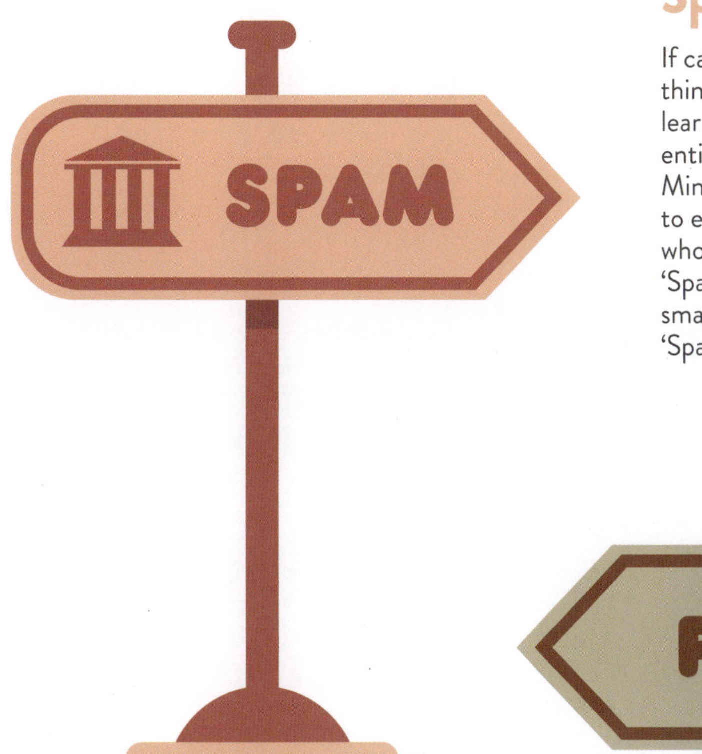

Spamples

If canned cooked pork is your thing, then you'll be excited to learn there's a museum devoted entirely to **Spam** in Austin, Minnesota, USA. And it's free to enter. Volunteer guides who work there are known as 'Spambassadors' and offer visitors small bits of Spam known as 'Spamples'.

Poo knew?

In Richmond, Tasmania, Australia there's a museum that takes poo, farts and toilets very seriously. The **Pooseum** is on a serious mission to educate visitors about the fascinating world of poo. Displays include a fart machine, dinosaur poo and poo collections of animals from all over the world. There are even 'PooTube' videos.

YOUR KITCHEN IS DIRTIER THAN YOUR TOILET SEAT

You might be better off making your salad on your toilet seat than preparing it in your kitchen. People disinfect their toilet seats all the time to destroy harmful bacteria, but they don't often apply the same levels of hygiene to the many different things in their kitchens. There are hidden germs lying in wait all around the room you prepare your food in.

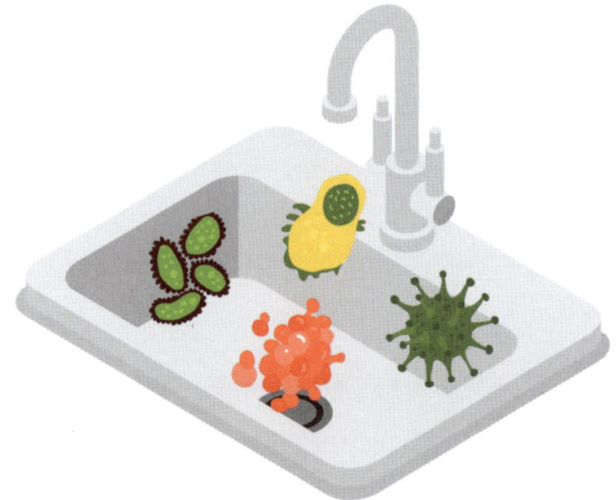

Dish the dirt

Because dishcloths and sponges get wet and stay moist, bacteria thrive and can grow like crazy on them. Alarmingly, they have the most harmful E. coli and other poo-based bacteria than anywhere else in the house. And to make matters even more disgusting, these cleaning items often remain around for way longer than they should, before we finally replace them.

Sink to the bottom

Sinks are much like dishcloths and sponges: they are both wet and moist. As further fuel for bacteria, there's also the food that's left on dishes and plates in the sink and put down the drain. This creates a breeding ground for harmful E. coli, which can make you extremely sick.

Cuts both ways

The average cutting board has **200 times** more fecal bacteria from raw meat than a toilet seat. Cutting boards are often just rinsed and left, but poultry and raw meat can leave behind salmonella and diseases that will give you diarrhea.

Rock bottom

The bottom shelf of a fridge is fertile ground for bacteria. Moisture and condensation drip down the shelves from above. Defrosting meat will often drip down onto fresh produce stored at the fridge's bottom, leading to contamination and illness.

Over the counter

The countertops in kitchens are often wiped down with the sponges and dishcloths from the sink – the same items that we already know can carry harmful bacteria. This means that when you do this, all you're doing is spreading germs over the countertop.

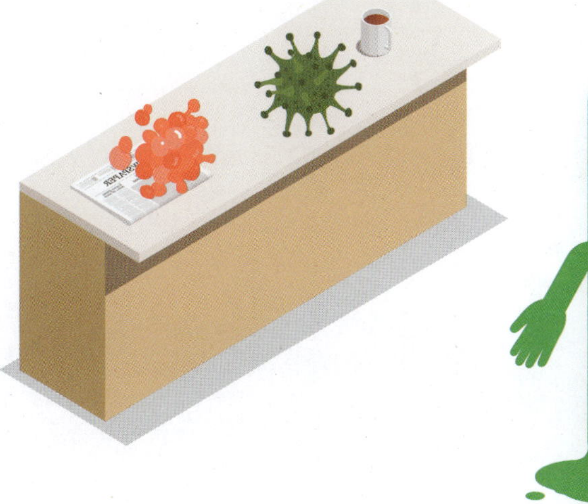

Mobile phones are one of the dirtiest objects you come into contact with every day. They are **10 times** dirtier than a toilet seat.

100 METRES

The height of the guano mound inside the **Deer Cave**, Sarawak, Malaysia.

COLOSSAL CAVES FULL OF POO

Caves are often wet, slimy and dark – gross! But there are caves all around the world that are even more disgusting, whose bat inhabitants both live there and use them as a giant toilet. One by one, each batty bowel movement eventually forms an enormous stinking pile of poo, often many metres high.

A pile of poo

Another name for the accumulated bat poo is **guano**, and although revolting, it's incredibly useful. As a manure, guano is a highly effective fertiliser and contains key nutrients essential for plant growth, such as nitrogen, phosphate, and potassium.

Dinner time

The insects in the caves also find a use for guano, especially the cockroaches. Hundreds of thousands of them completely cover the giant poo piles, like a repulsive insect carpet, and feed from it, making it appear as if the mound is moving and alive.

Blow up

It's not just fertiliser that guano is used for; it's also handy if you want to blow something up. It consists mainly of potassium nitrate, a key ingredient in explosives. In **1812**, United States soldiers used guano for gunpowder, and in the First World War soldiers dried guano for bombs.

20 MILLION

The estimated number of bats living in the **Bracken Cave**, Comal County, Texas, USA. This is the world's largest bat colony.

THE MOST POLLUTED PLACE ON EARTH

The South Asian country **Bangladesh** is famous for many things. For one, it's home to the world's largest river delta, where Bengal tigers proudly roam. It also has the longest natural uninterrupted sea beach in the whole of Asia, Cox's Bazar beach, which is **150 kilometres** long. But one aspect of Bangladesh that you won't find in the tourism brochures is that it's currently the most polluted country in the entire world.

Up in the air

Bangladesh is the most polluted place on Earth because of **air pollution**. Even though it's only the eighth largest country in the world, with a population of **165 million**, when it comes to air quality, Bangladesh has the worst in the world.

Brick it up

The sources for Bangladesh's atrocious air quality are brick-burning kilns, vehicle exhausts, different industries, open waste burning and large-scale construction.

28%

This is the estimated percentage of deaths in Bangladesh from diseases caused by pollution.

Indoors and outdoors

The pollution is problematic both outdoors and indoors. Indoor air pollution is actually one of the biggest killers of Bangladeshi people. On average, **113,000** people die annually from it, compared to **15,000** who die from outdoor air pollution.

7

This is the number of years that your life expectancy is reduced by living in Bangladesh.

KILOGRAMS

This is the weight of pooed-out sand that an individual parrotfish produces each year.

HAWAII'S WHITE SANDY BEACHES ARE MADE OF FISH POO

Hawaii is beautiful. It's warm, it's welcoming and its beaches are famous all around the world for their clear turquoise waters and immaculate white sand. It's basically paradise. But the origin of that pristine white sand is anything but blissful. That wonderful white sand is made up mostly of fish poo. The poo from **parrotfish** to be precise. And lots of it.

No stomach for it

Parrotfish have two sets of teeth but have no stomachs. What this means is the chewed-up dead coral travels straight through them and emerges from the fish in a wisp of white smoke as it is pooed out into the ocean.

Algae back

The striking beautiful blue and yellow parrotfish live on coral reefs located around tropical places like Hawaii. They love nothing more than chomping down on dead coral, which removes excess algae and helps to revitalise the ecosystem of the reef.

Tossed around

This new pooed sand collects over time on the ocean floor and then gets tossed around by the swell, resulting in the wonderful white-sand beaches.

1000

This is the number of teeth each parrotfish has. They are made of fluorapatite, one of the hardest biominerals in the world. Harder even than copper, gold and silver.

GROSSOMETER

THERE ARE FROZEN BODIES ALL OVER MOUNT EVEREST

Mount Everest holds the official title of Earth's highest mountain above sea level and attracts many climbers, including highly experienced mountaineers. But not everybody who attempts to climb to its summit makes it to the top, let alone makes it home to tell the tale. Many climbers have failed to return from the world's highest mountain, earning it another title, albeit an unofficial one. It is 'the world's highest graveyard' as the frozen bodies of the climbers now litter the famous mountain.

Well preserved

Due to the temperature, these corpses remain frozen all year round, leaving them almost perfectly preserved. The still-frozen body of **George Mallory** was discovered in **1999**. It had barely decayed at all, even though he and his climbing partner disappeared over **80 years** ago.

Find your way

Although very much dead, the bodies now have a morbid practical use as the frozen corpses act as wayfinders for any climbers attempting to reach the mountain's summit.

Rainbow Alley

There is an area of Mount Everest with the alluring name of **Rainbow Alley**, but what lies there is anything but. The site is littered with the dead bodies of unsuccessful climbers, all wearing blue, red, orange and green jackets. From a distance, it looks so colourful, like a rainbow.

Green boots

Perhaps the most famous frozen body on Everest is '**Green Boots**', named after the green climbing boots still on the body. They are believed by many to be that of **Tsewang Paljor**, an Indian climber who died on Everest in **1996**.

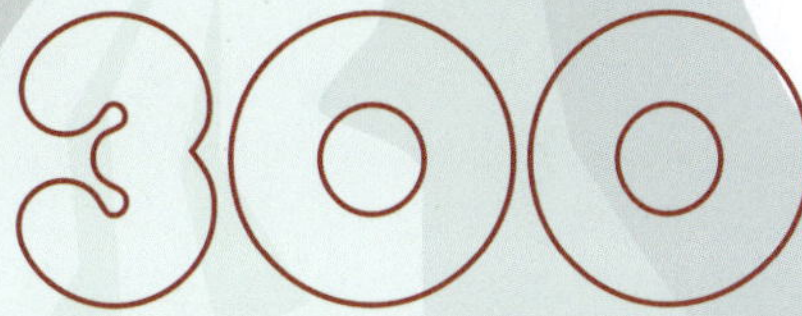

This is the number of climbers who have failed to return alive after attempting to climb Mount Everest. Many of these bodies are still on the mountain.

Break free

The average weight of a frozen dead body on Everest is **90 kilograms**. The bodies become frozen to the mountainside in just an hour and completely frozen solid in just four hours. Most are left where they are, but those that are moved must first be broken free from the mountainside.

THE STINGING PLANT THAT MAKES YOU VOMIT

Australia is home to many animals that would happily end your life. But as well as sharks, spiders, jellyfish and snakes, Australia is also home to a terrifyingly dangerous plant – Dendrocnide moroides, or the **Gympie-Gympie** plant. It's covered in tiny stinging hairs which, if touched, deliver a potent neurotoxin that instantly penetrates your skin. What follows is a stinging sensation that's been described as like being burned with acid and being electrocuted – at the same time. The pain can remain like this for anywhere from days to years!

The suicide plant

Gympie-Gympie is also called the 'suicide plant'. The agonising sting can last so long that some victims eventually take their own lives to avoid the pain.

Tight fit

Any attempt to remove the stinging hairs is almost impossible as they are too tightly packed to pluck out with tweezers. For the sake of retaining your sanity, and even your life, the Gympie-Gympie is best to be avoided!

If you're stung by the Gympie-Gympie, you'll need to grab a sick bag because you'll instantly vomit.

THE SMELLIEST PLACES ON EARTH

Seal Island is a small land mass located **5.7 kilometres** off the northern beaches of False Bay, near Cape Town in South Africa. As its name suggests, the island is home to a large colony of Cape fur seals. Seabirds have made it their home too, despite there being no vegetation on the island and no soil either. It doesn't even have a beach. But what it does have is rotting seal flesh, rotting fish and lots and lots of poo. These repellant ingredients create a smell so rancid that Seal Island lays claim to being one of the smelliest places on Earth.

70,000

This is the number of **Cape fur seals** that occupy Seal Island.

Nasal assault

The complicated sewer system of **Mexico City** is one of the worst smelling in the world. It's prone to flooding, which makes the stench even worse. The rotting, corrosive, toxic sewage is so horrendous it's been described as being like an assault on people's nostrils.

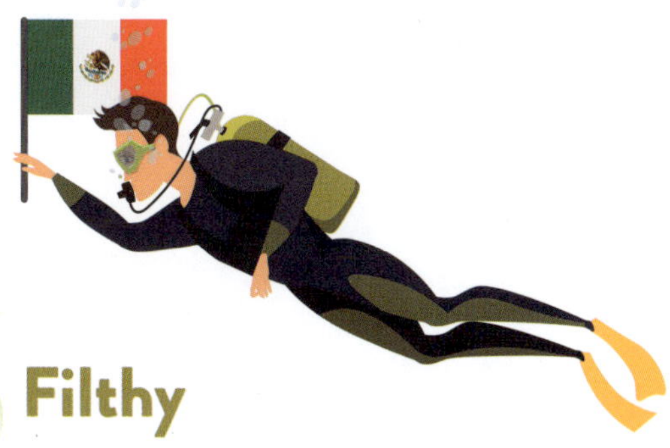

Filthy

Sewer divers in Mexico City are employed to repair pumps and remove blockages. They work in total darkness because the filth they're swimming in is so thick. They cannot even see their own hands in front of them and have to rely on their sense of touch and memory to navigate the stinking sewers.

Because of all the seals, the island attracts **great white sharks**, often seen hurling themselves out of the water with seals gripped tightly in their mouths.

MAKING SECRET STINK BOMBS

Stink bombs are gross, but great fun. And if there's one thing better than a stink bomb, it's a stink bomb that people won't even know is there – a secret stink bomb. You can easily make one using a normal balloon and any smelly ingredient. Fish sauce is ideal. Inflated and tied balloons always deflate slowly over time as the tiny air molecules inside move through the skin of the balloon. This is known as diffusion. Air will always diffuse from an area of higher pressure to an area of lower pressure. A balloon that's been inflated has greater air pressure inside it, so the air gradually diffuses into the lower air pressure that surrounds the balloon. The same applies to any scent molecules you put inside it. The scent molecules will escape from the balloon and diffuse into the room around it. No one will suspect it was the balloon causing the room to stink. Very sneaky!

What you will need

Funnel

Balloon

1 teaspoon fish sauce

How to make the stink bomb

1. Put the funnel into the balloon.
2. Pour the fish sauce into the funnel and shake it down into the balloon.
3. Remove the funnel.
4. Carefully inflate and tie the balloon.
5. Put the balloon in the room you want to stink out.
6. Sit back and after about 30 minutes enjoy the pong as people slowly start to realise there's an awful smell in the room somewhere.

Other smelly ingredients that would work well inside the balloons are **garlic**, **cheese** and **yoghurt**.

THE DESERTED ISLAND FULL OF CREEPY DECAYING DOLLS

An island with decaying old dolls strung up in trees sounds like something from a dark fairy tale or a horror film, but **La Isla de las Muñecas** (The Island of the Dolls) is very real. Located in **Xochimilco**, south of the centre of **Mexico City**, the island draws curious visitors from all over the world.

GROSSOMETER

Spirited away

The dolls were originally hung by a recluse called **Julian Santana**. He was the only resident on the island until he passed away. He claims to have one day discovered the body of a young girl and her doll in the canal. He hung the first doll to appease the girl's spirit and then carried on adding more until his death.

1500

This is estimated number of dolls on the island.

THE PARASITIC FUNGUS THAT CONTROLS THE MINDS OF ANTS

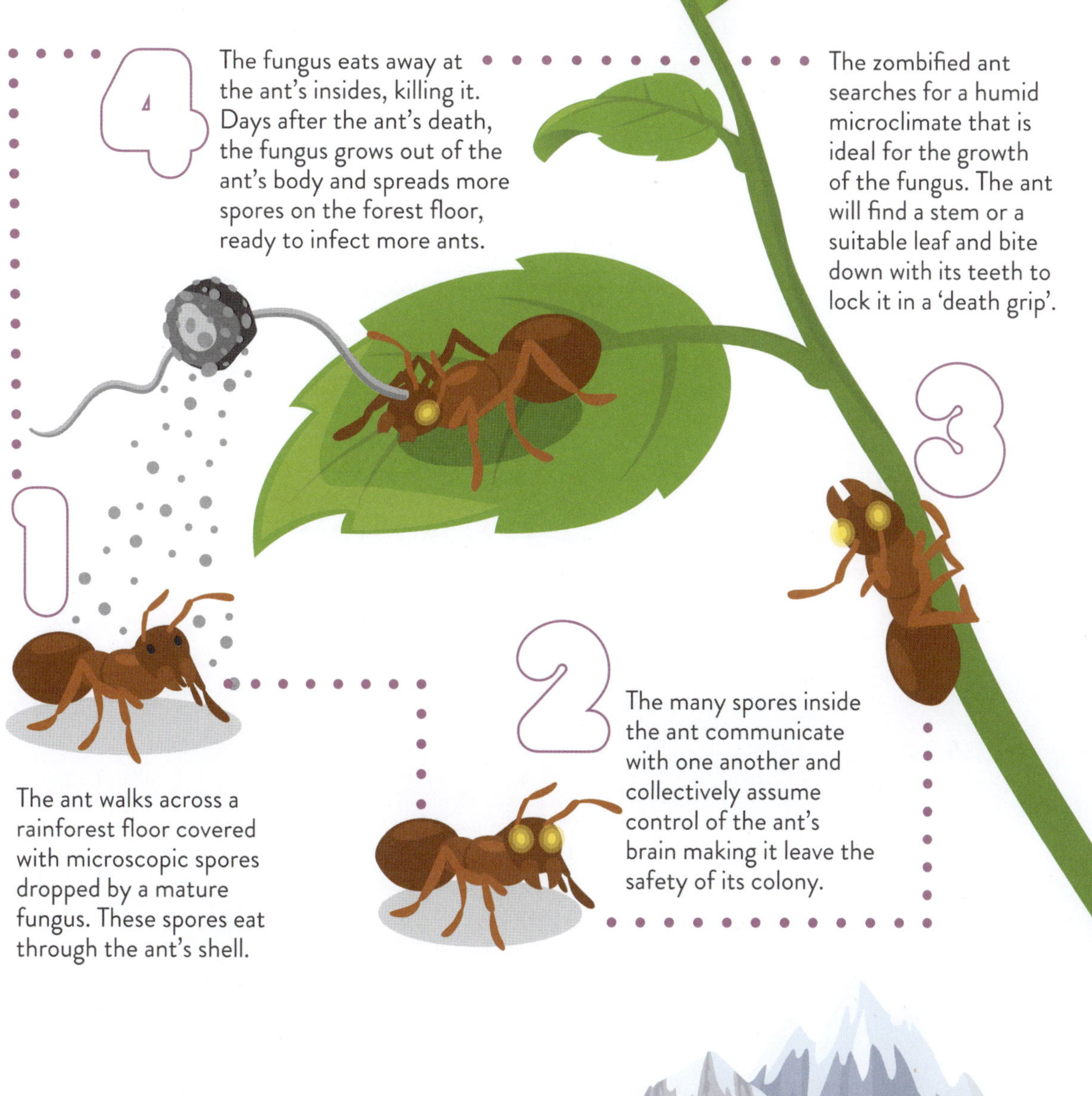

Carpenter ant versus **fungus** doesn't sound like a fair match-up. After all, carpenter ants are fairly big (for ants), they travel in large groups and those razor-sharp mandibles have a powerful bite. But there is a fungus called **Ophiocordyceps unilateralis**, or 'zombie-ant fungus' as it's more commonly known, that not only destroys carpenter ants with a deadly pathogen, but in doing so takes over their insect minds.

Old timers

There's evidence that the fungus that makes real-life zombies and convinces them to stagger to their death has existed for quite some time – **48 million years** to be exact. This makes the fungus older even than the rise of the Himalayas.

The coffee tree

The coffee tree (Coffea) is an evergreen flowering plant found in tropical Africa and Asia..

The coffee fruit

The plant grows coffee cherries. They contain caffeine as a way of defending themselves against animals eating them.

The Luwak

The **Luwak** (Palm Civet Cat) loves the ripest coffee cherries and eats as many as they can find.

THE WORLD'S MOST EXPENSIVE COFFEE IS MADE WITH CAT POO

The drinking

The coffee beans are used to brew a cup of very expensive coffee. They are said to have a very distinctive flavour. It's no wonder!

Unfortunately, farmers today are keeping **Luwaks** in tiny cages on coffee plantations that fail to meet animal welfare standards for hygiene, shelter and mobility – a good enough reason to avoid buying their expensive beans.

The coffee beans

Workers handpick the coffee beans out of the poo and wash, dry and roast them.

The pooing

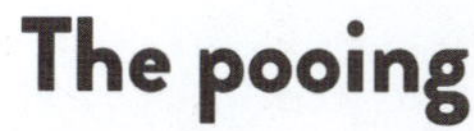

About a day later, the Luwak goes to the toilet and their poos are then collected by farmers.

The digestion

The **Luwak** partially digests the coffee cherries, which removes the chaff and leaves behind partially fermented coffee seeds, which we call 'beans'.

When you think of luxurious and expensive foods, cat poo coffee is probably not the first thing that springs to mind. But **Luwak coffee** (kopi Luwak) is exactly that: coffee that has been harvested from the poo of a South East Asian jungle cat called the **Luwak** (Palm Civet Cat). The coffee is made from coffee cherries that have been eaten, digested, and pooped out by the small creature that looks like a cross between a cat and a raccoon. A cup of Luwak coffee can be 60 times more expensive than an average cup of coffee.

30 YEARS

This is the age of the chewing gum wall.

15 METRES

This is the current length of the chewing gum wall, but as people keep adding to it every day it continues to grow.

THE GIANT WALL COVERED IN CHEWING GUM

Since the early 1990s, a wall just outside the main entrance to **Pike Place Market** in Seattle has slowly been getting covered by hundreds of thousands of pieces of used **chewing gum**. And that number is still growing. The wall has become a giant, sticky, gooey mess that people come from far and wide to visit and leave their own gum on.

1065 KILOGRAMS

This is the weight of gum that was removed in 2015. It took over **130 hours** to do so and was the first time the wall had been cleaned in **20 years**.

On hot days, the stench from the old chewing gum is horrendous.

Germ of an idea

The wall has been voted one of the **top 5 germiest tourist attractions** in the whole world, so if you do ever touch it or even leave your gum there you should probably wash your hands afterwards.

LET'S
DO
THIS!

MAKING YOUR PEE SMELL

Have you ever eaten asparagus and then afterwards, when you've gone to the toilet, noticed a funny, unpleasant scent coming from your pee? If you have, you're not the only one. The reason for this is **aspargusic acid**, which is found exclusively in asparagus. When the asparagus is digested, asparagusic acid breaks down into sulphur-containing byproducts. Sulphur has a stinky smell, hence the pongy pee. The following experiment is a brilliantly simple way to test and observe this. Happy peeing!

Asparagus pee usually shows up between **15** and **30 minutes** after the vegetable has been eaten and can last for several hours – sometimes for up to **14 hours**! Not everybody who eats asparagus will have smelly pee though. Somewhere between **20%** and **50%** of people will experience it.

What you will need

Asparagus (boiled, steamed or fried)

1 glass water

Toilet

How to make your pee smell

1. Eat the asparagus (it's good for you).
2. Drink the water (that's good for you too).
3. When you're ready, go to the toilet and observe how your pee smells.
4. Record how long this pungent pee phenomenon last for.

OYSTER MUSHROOMS ARE CARNIVOROUS AND HUNT THEIR PREY

Oyster mushrooms are commonly seen in supermarkets and grocery stores. You often see them as pizza toppings too. They're beautiful and extremely delicious. The shell-shaped fungi grow in amazing clusters on dead trees or stumps all over the world. But these fantastic fungi harbour a dark secret: they eat meat, and hunt and trap it too!

Mushrooms are more closely related to people than plants. Animals and fungi share a common ancestor and branched away from plants around **1.5 billion years** ago. Animals and fungi then separated a little more recently but still over **1 billion years** ago.

Can of worms

Oyster mushrooms' food of choice are **Nematodes**, also called roundworms. These are small creatures made of flesh and complete with guts, nerves and muscles. They are very much alive.

Toxic avenger

The murderous mushrooms first lure and trap their prey by releasing chemicals that smell like food to the worm. They then paralyse the squirming sufferer within minutes by injecting a liquid toxin into the worm before dissolving its corpse and absorbing the resulting slurry.

Food for thought

The dead trees the oyster mushrooms grow on have limited access to nitrogen. The mushrooms eat the worms to consume their protein-rich nitrogen.

200

This is the number of mushroom species that are considered carnivorous. But only the oyster mushroom hunts and traps its prey.

Pleased to meat you

Carnivorous mushrooms may be one of the only vegan and vegetarian foods that eats meat.

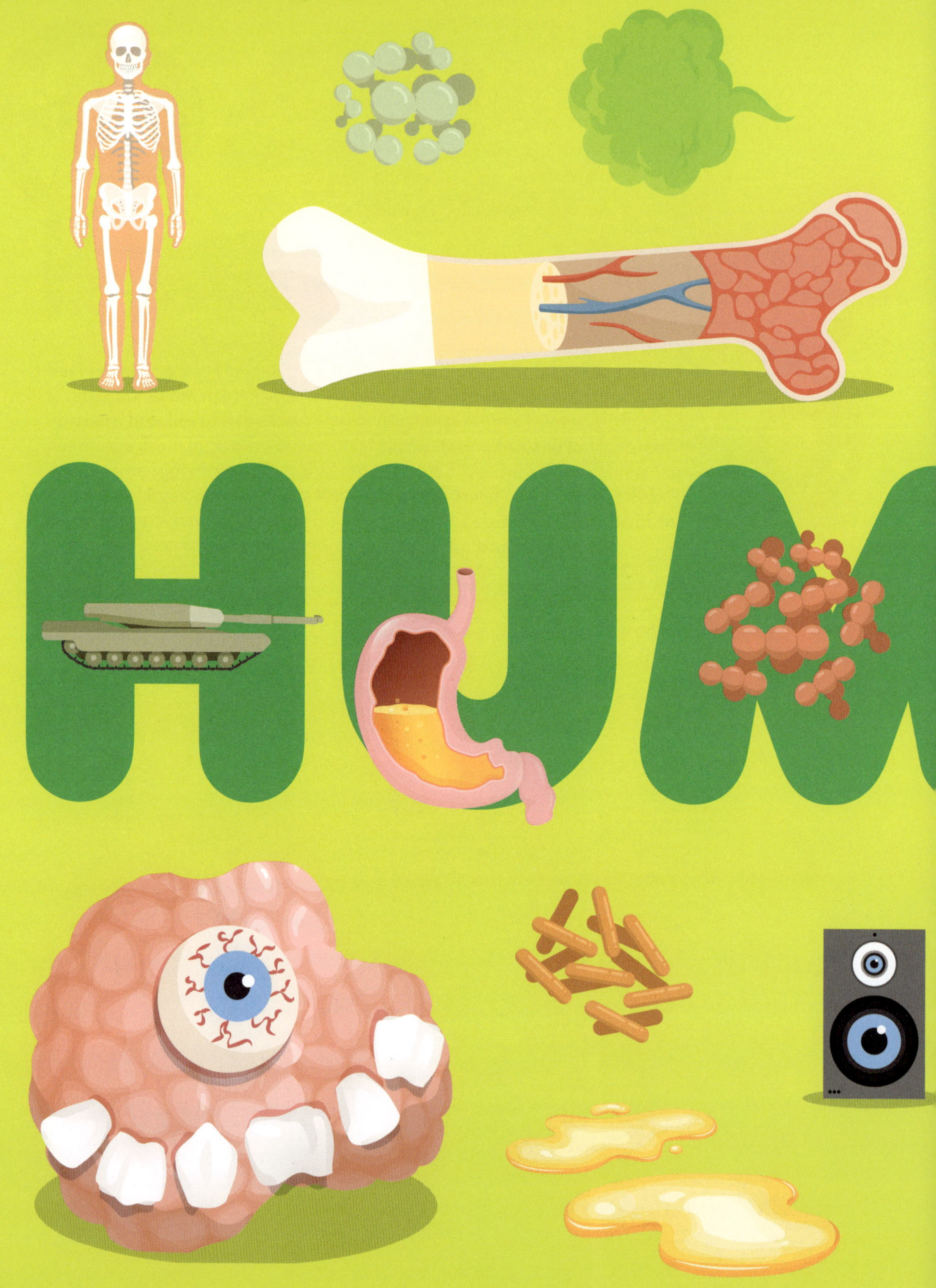
HUM

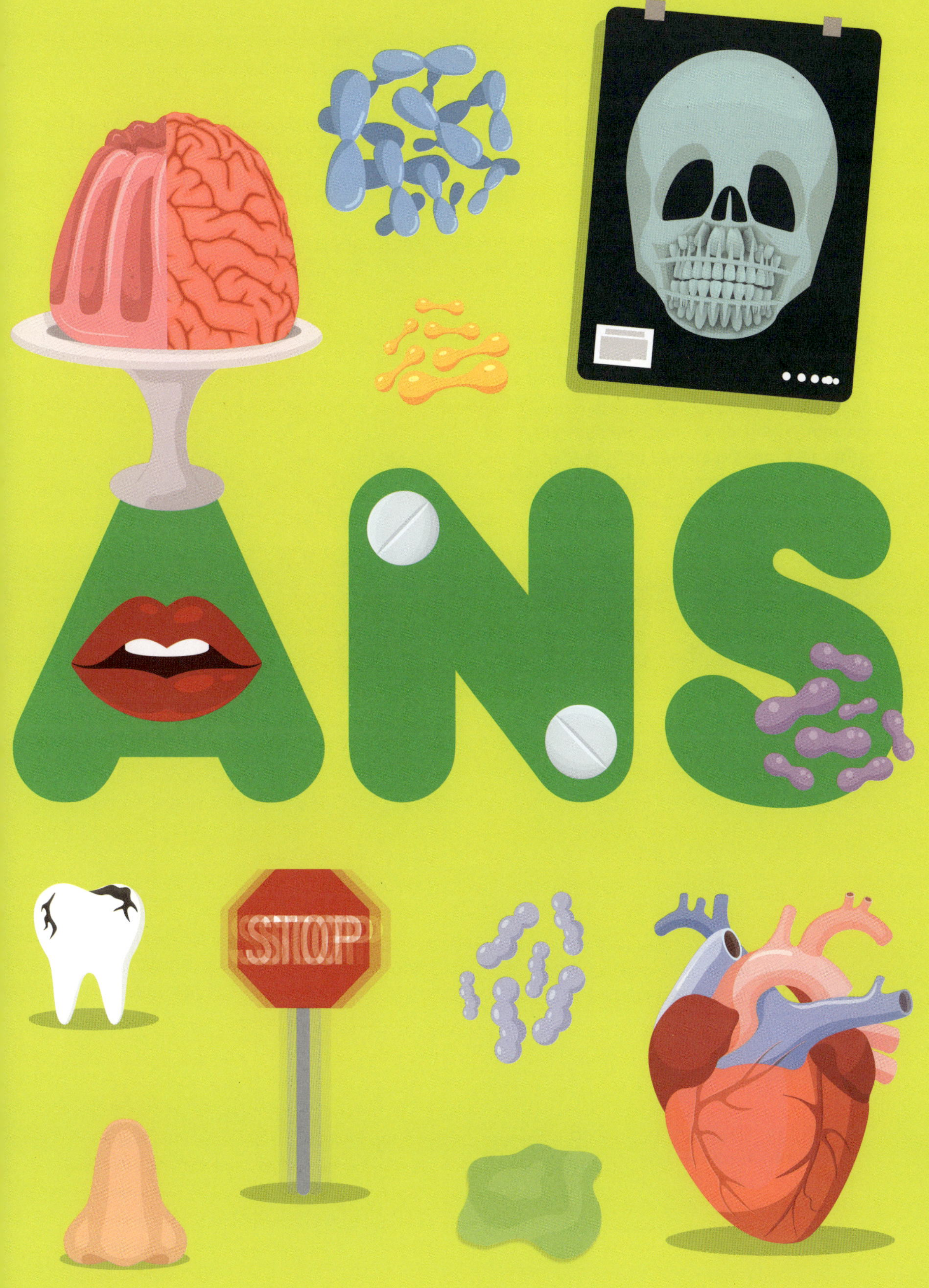
ANS
STOP

THERE IS A RAINFOREST OF SPECIES INSIDE YOUR BELLY BUTTON

How often do you clean your belly button? Be honest now. Our belly buttons are one of the most rarely scrubbed places on our bodies. We somehow seem to forget they're even there, especially if you have an 'innie' and not an 'outie'. This intermittent attitude to cleaning allows a flourishing and diverse ecosystem of microbes to exist. It's a jungle in there!

2368

This is the number of bacterial species that were found when scientists examined **60** belly buttons.

1458

This is the number of bacterial species that may be new to science that were discovered in those **60** examined belly buttons.

Fungi and fluff

As well as bacteria, our belly buttons can also contain fungi and fluff.

Smelly cheese

If our belly buttons get infected, things can get rather smelly as they might also contain a foul-smelling, cheese-like liquid

Your belly button is your first-ever scar. The scar tissue is formed from when your umbilical cord was cut not long after your birth.

YOU WILL DROOL ENOUGH IN YOUR LIFETIME TO FILL TWO SWIMMING POOLS

Have you ever woken up in the morning to find your pillow has a huge wet patch from the previous night's drooling session? It's strange as you have no recollection of it happening, but the evidence of your slobbering is right there in front of you. Drooling is something we do all the time, and over the course of your lifetime you'll produce an amazing amount of saliva – enough to fill two standard-size swimming pools!

Bad breath

Saliva is produced by glands in your mouth and keeps your mouth moist and comfortable. It helps you chew, taste and swallow, as well as fights the germs in your mouth, preventing bad breath. Too little saliva can result in bad breath and food tasting differently.

You produce enough saliva in just **1 year** to fill up **2** bathtubs.

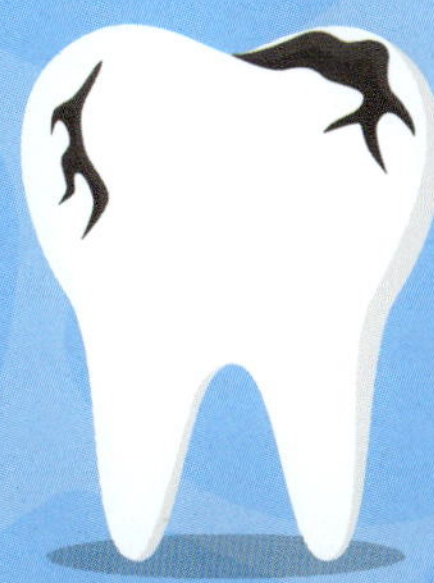

750

MILLILITRES

This is the amount of saliva the average person produces in a **single day**. Enough to fill a wine bottle.

The acid test

Saliva helps keep the pH balance of your mouth slightly alkaline. And it's a good job too because if it didn't, your mouth would become acidic and would dissolve your own teeth.

25,000

LITRES

This is the amount of saliva the average person produces in a lifetime.

Sealed with a kiss

When you deeply kiss someone, you exchange saliva with them and the millions of bacteria contained within it. A **10-second** kiss will transfer around **80 million** bacteria.

YOU CANNOT HOLD A FART UNTIL IT DISAPPEARS

If you've ever been in a situation where you've successfully managed to hold in a fart for fear of embarrassment, then it might come as a surprise to learn that you didn't. That fart got out. Just very slowly. The science behind a fart is quite straightforward. A fart is a bubble of gas, and ultimately there's nowhere for it to go besides out of your bum. It only seemed to vanish because you stopped thinking about it, but the truth is it just escaped gradually without you even realising it.

Everybody farts

Everybody farts. Everybody. And anyone who tells you differently is telling a lie. The number of farts we all do daily is, on average, between **10** and **20**. That's a lot of farts!

A beautiful thing

Farts are very misunderstood. People tend to think of them as a bad thing, but in most cases, they're the byproduct of a very beautiful thing – the complex ecosystem of living bacteria that calls your intestines home.

On average you fart enough in one day to fill a party balloon. That's about **700 millilitres.**

Smell you later

The reason you don't find your own farts as bad as those of other people is because you get used to your own fart smell, just as you get used to your own smells in general. That's why you might notice a scent walking into someone else's home, but not your own.

MAKING A FART DIARY

If you've ever been curious as to how many farts you do in a day, or a week, or perhaps even in a year, a great way to look at it scientifically is to keep a **fart diary**. You'll need to keep track of what you're eating and what effect it has on you, and then write it all down. Observe and report! The diary on the opposite page is perfect for this, so make your own copies of it and get scribbling. Just make sure you have one nearby after eating any beans.

Foods that make you fart like crazy include **broccoli, cauliflower**, **oats**, **whole wheat bread**, **milk**, **cheese**, **yoghurt**, **apples**, **bananas**, **peaches**, **beans** and **fizzy drinks**. Even **chewing gum** can make you super gassy.

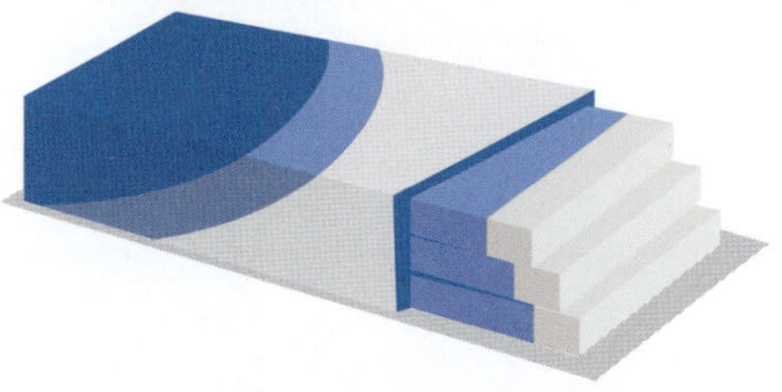

MY FART DIARY

DATE

MY FOOD

BREAKFAST ....

LUNCH ....

DINNER ....

SNACKS ....

MY FARTS

How bad did it smell?

TIME	LENGTH	SOUND	SMELL

RESULTS What foods made you fart and when?

CONCLUSION What do you now know about your farting routine?

YOUNG CHILDREN'S SKULLS HAVE A FULL SET OF TEETH

You're a tooth-manufacturing factory. Your teeth start to grow even before you're born and over the course of your lifetime you'll have 20 baby (or milk) teeth and, once they've fallen out, 32 permanent teeth to take their place. However, there's a time in your life when you still have all your milk teeth and your permanent teeth are concealed inside your young skull, patiently lying in wait for their time to erupt through your gums and take their place in your jaw. Thankfully, we can't see them as they're all hidden inside your skull, below your eyes and in your chin. What a terrifying image!

This is the number of teeth that were found crammed inside the mouth of a 7-year-old Indian boy. They were inside a 'bag-like-mass', and were carefully removed by surgeons. It took the medical team 5 hours to carefully search through and count them all.

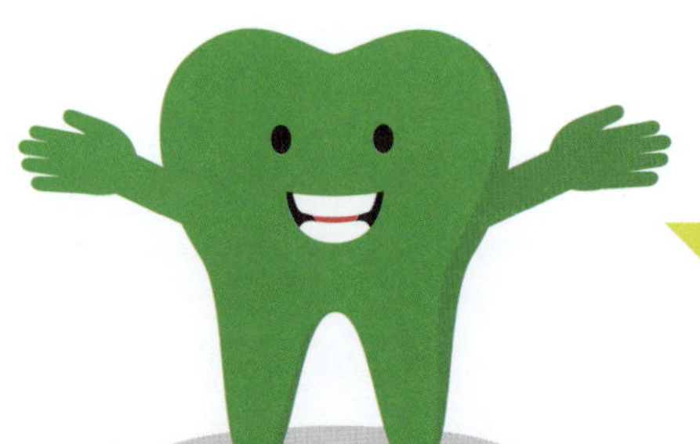

If you got a toothache in the Middle Ages, they would treat it by inserting live caterpillars into your mouth. Another 'remedy' was to put hot wax into your mouth. Ouch!

Fall into decay

Tooth decay is one of the most prevalent diseases in the world, second only to the common cold. It's at least **5 times** more frequent than asthma and fevers and if left untreated can create some serious health problems and in very rare cases, death!

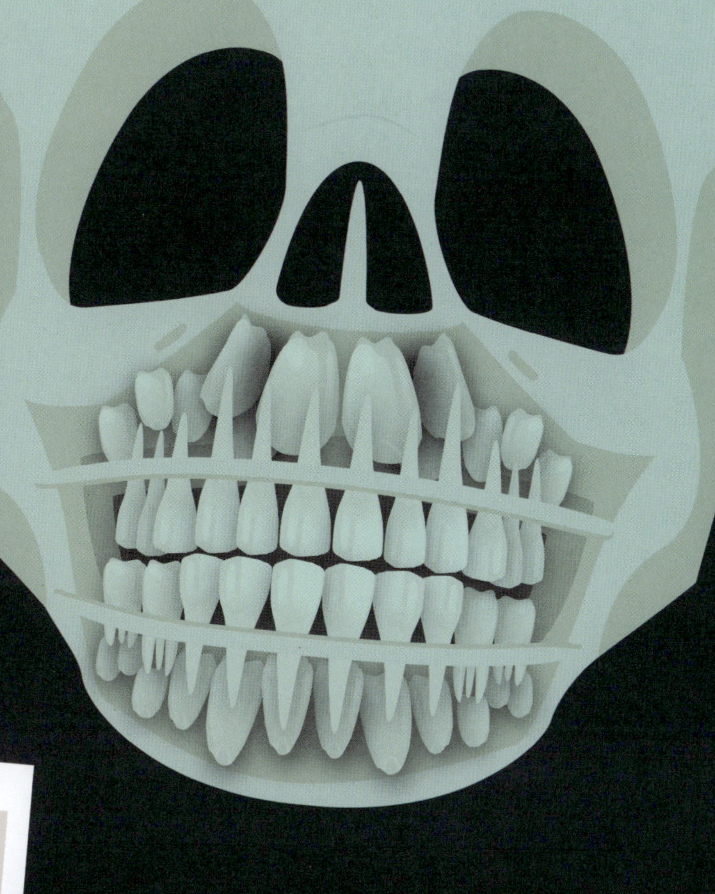

You carry around **2 kilograms** of bacteria in and on your body.

YOUR BODY IS FILLED WITH FRIENDLY BACTERIA THAT WILL ONE DAY EAT YOU

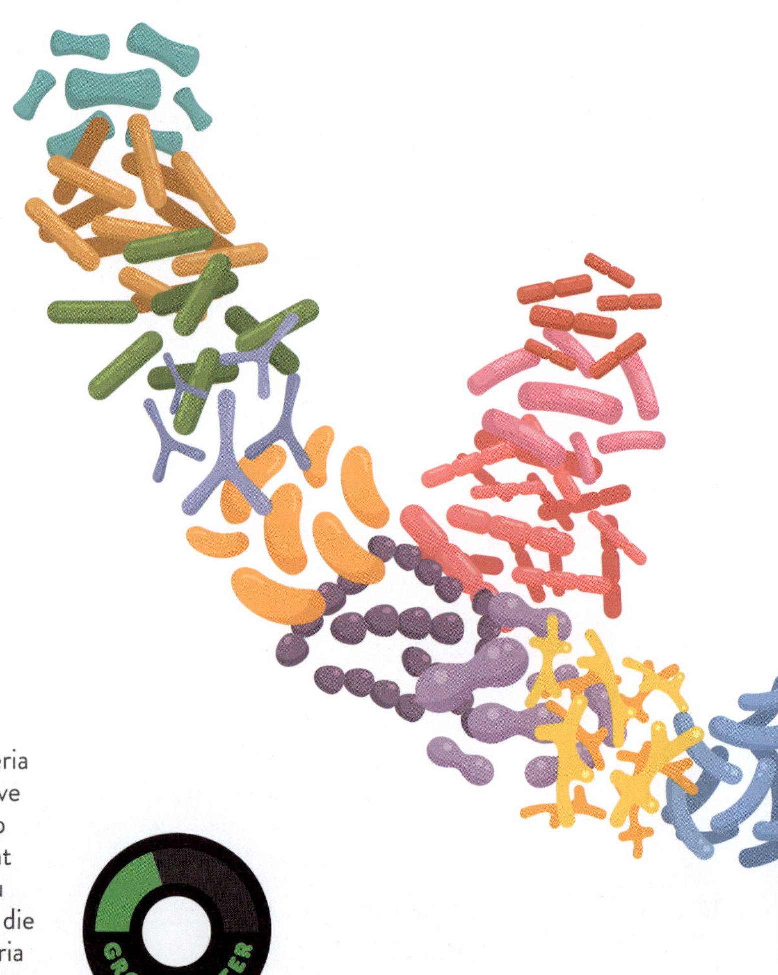

You are both covered with bacteria and filled with them too. You have a friendly, symbiotic relationship with the bacteria in your gut that keeps you healthy and helps you digest food. However, once you die a whole lot of your body's bacteria are going to swoop in and they're going to chow down. On you!

GROSSOMETER

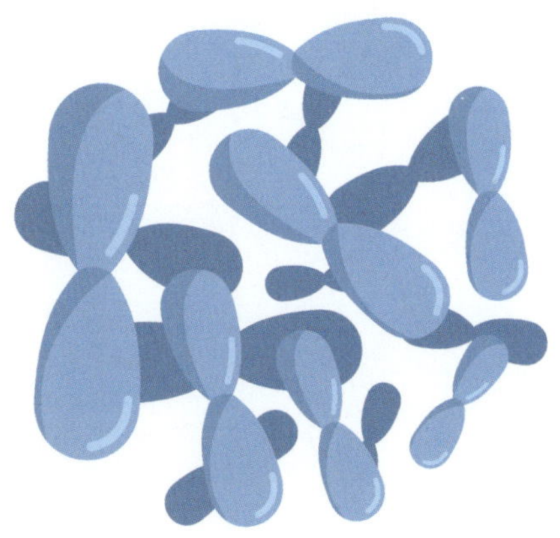

Battle to the death

When you're alive, your human cells are waging an epic and long-fought lifelong battle to the death with bacterial cells. If you're healthy, your cells have the winning advantage. Decomposition happens when your cells finally lose.

First up

The microbes in your intestines get to dine first. As soon as you pop your clogs, they'll start decomposing you from the inside out. On the outside of your body, the bacteria on your skin start their mission to break in. It's an all-out attack.

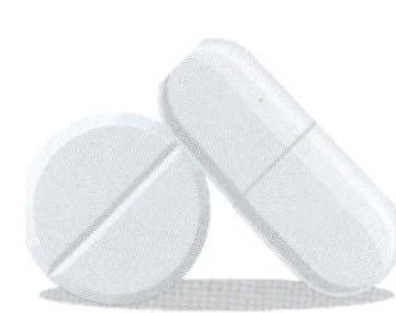

The resistance

If bacteria start to win the war while you're alive, this is called **infection**. Your options are to either physically remove the invaders by cleaning a wound or use **antibiotics** to poison them. Due to an overuse of antibiotics, bacteria have become resistant to these weapons, and they are now sometimes failing, leading to further infections, illness, and even death.

YOUR EYELASHES HAVE MITES LIVING IN THEM

Worm into

Demodex look like stubby little worms, with a cigar-shaped tail and stumpy legs at the other end, but they are **arachnids**, similar to ticks and spiders.

Bad hair day

Eyelashes aren't the only place you'll find these creepy creatures; they live all over your body, anywhere there's a hair follicle. They flourish on the natural oils produced by your face, where they crawl, eat and reproduce.

Creepy little creatures crawling on your eyelashes sounds like the stuff of make-believe – but it's very true. Your eyelashes have mites called **Demodex**, and they are right now feasting on your dead skin cells and oil. But before you rush off and examine your eyelashes in the mirror, you should know that these mites are microscopic and you can't see them with the naked eye. Depending on the species, they're only about **0.15** to **0.4** mm in length. That's about the size of half a grain of salt.

Dig in

Due to an aversion to light, Demodex aggressively burrow into eyelash follicles, leaving their tails sticking out. At night, they emerge and crawl all over your face, eating dead skin and looking for potential mates.

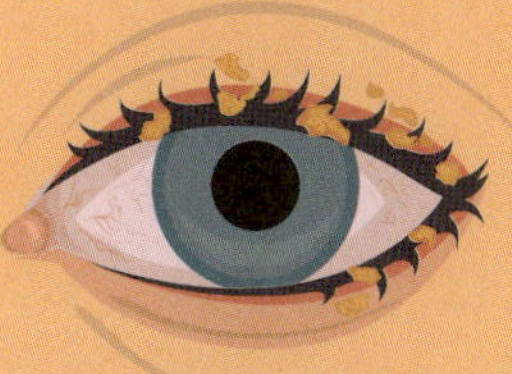

Mostly harmless

As gross as the idea of parasitic mites living on your eyelashes and face sounds, they are in fact harmless and are 'cleaning' your face of dead skin. Problems arise when you have too many of them and your eyes can become irritated and inflamed.

YOUR STOMACH IS CONSTANTLY BATTLING NOT TO EAT ITSELF

Your stomach digests pretty much everything that you send down to it. Tough fibrous plants? No problem. Meat? No problem. Bones? No problem too. It's able to do this by producing a fluid from its lining. This is **stomach acid**, or gastric acid, and it's highly acidic, which helps break down food to make it easier to digest. In fact, this acid is so powerful that your body needs to come up with a defence mechanism to protect itself, so that when your stomach acid is finished digesting your dinner it doesn't move onto eating your stomach for dessert!

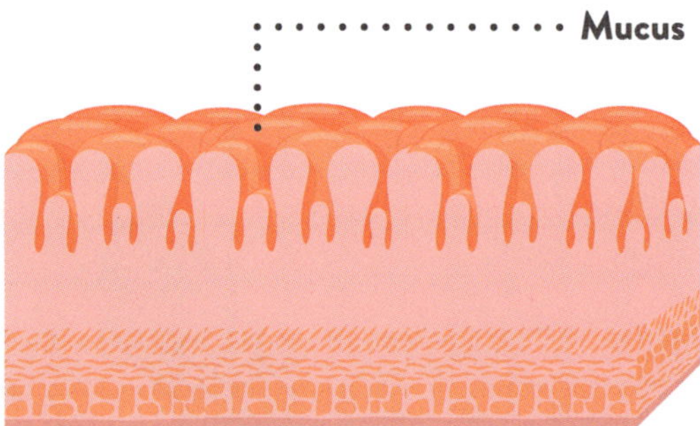

Mucus

The key to your stomach winning the war with the acid is **mucus**. Your stomach produces a protective layer of it that keeps the two battling sides apart with a special neutralising agent. The mucus also lubricates the food you've swallowed and is responsible for creating the enzymes that help your body digest proteins. Mucus may be gross, but it's absolutely amazing.

Ulcers

There are times when the mucus fails to protect the outer edge of the stomach and the acid wins this particular battle. This results in what we call **ulcers** and they are extremely painful.

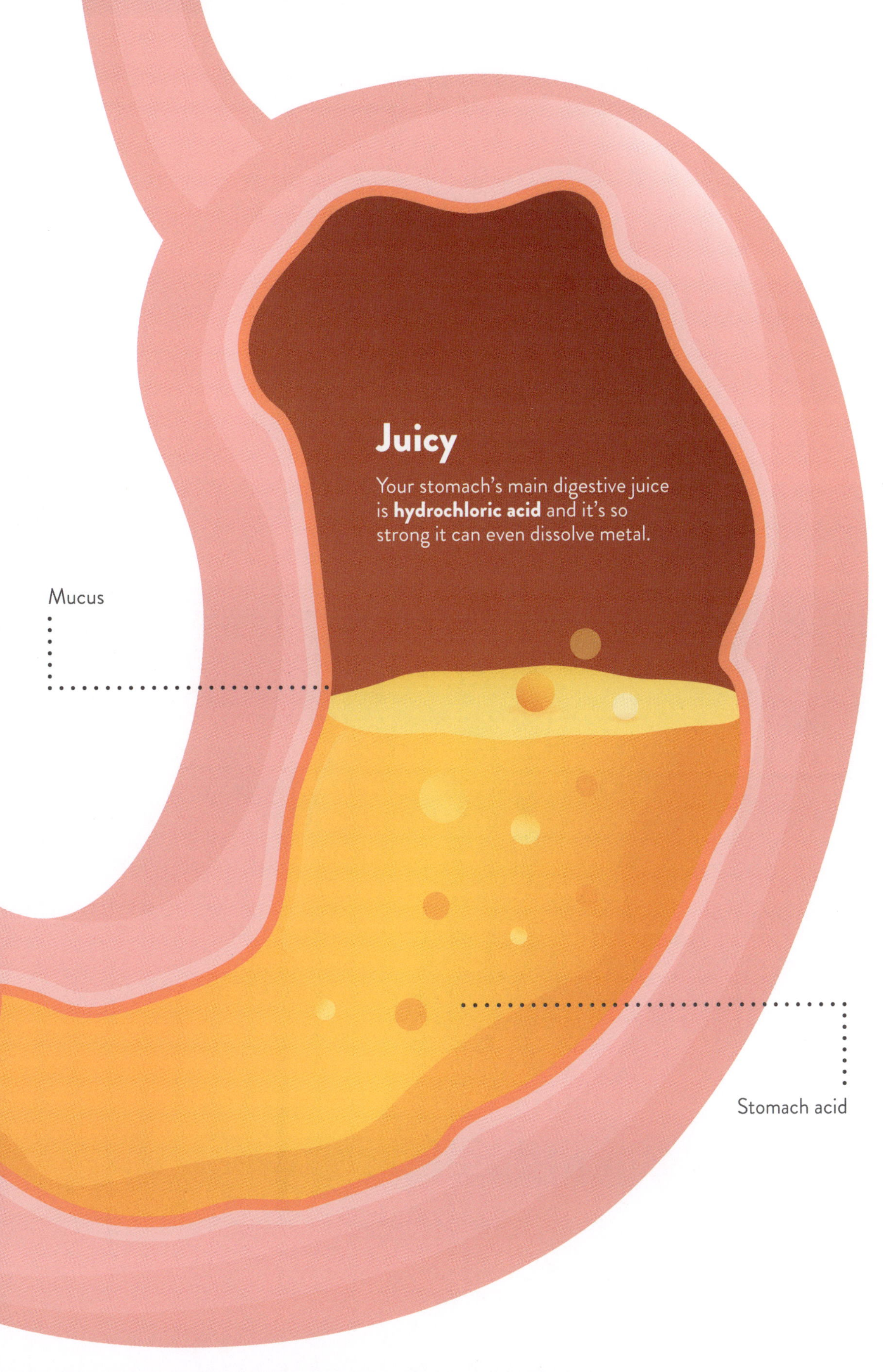
Juicy
Your stomach's main digestive juice is **hydrochloric acid** and it's so strong it can even dissolve metal.
Mucus
Stomach acid

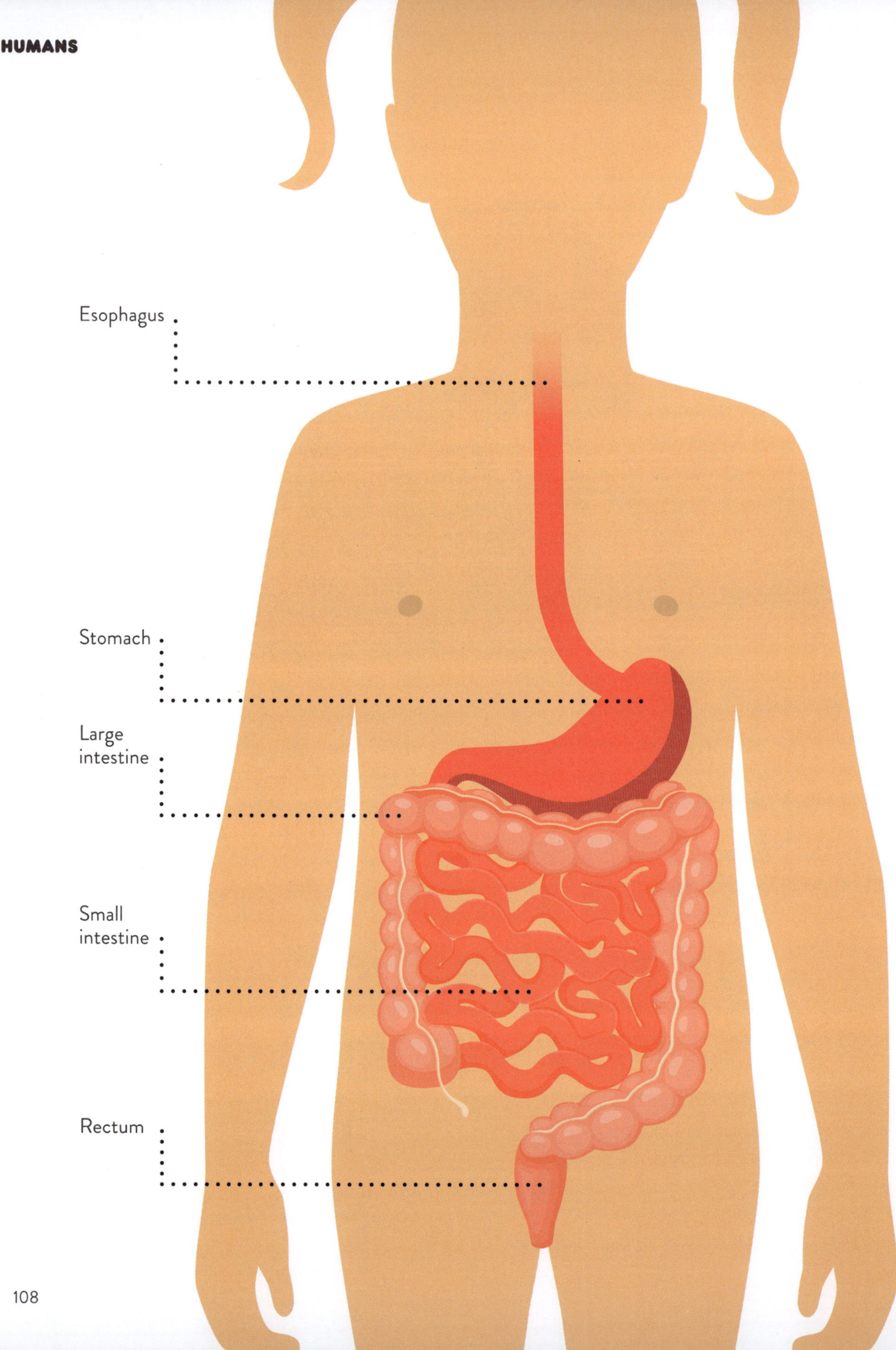
Esophagus
Stomach
Large
intestine
Small
intestine
Rectum

YOUR STOMACH IS NOT WHERE YOU THINK IT IS

People often satisfyingly pat their tummies, around the area of their belly buttons, to let you know that they are full, or have enjoyed their yummy meal. Well, next time you see this happen you can let them know that they are patting in the wrong spot. Your stomach is located much higher up your body than you realise. It is in fact closer to your nipples than it is to your belly button!

The organs that food and liquids travel through when they are swallowed, digested, absorbed and leave your body as poo, are called your **gastrointestinal tract**. They contain trillions of microbes, around **90 percent** of which are bacteria.

Musclehead

Your body doesn't rely on gravity to move swallowed food through it. Rather, it uses muscles that constrict and relax in a wavelike fashion to push the food along. This means you can still eat even if you're standing on your head! Please do not try this at home though.

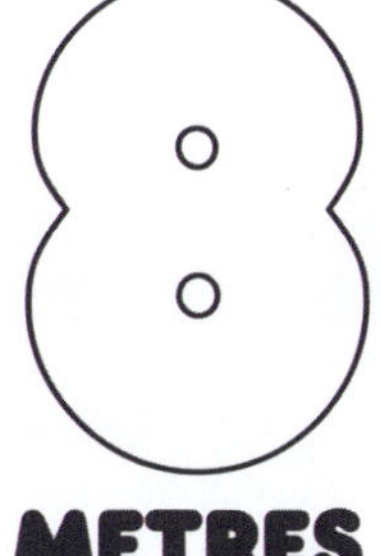

8 METRES

This is the average collective length of your small and large intestines. It's the same length as an **orca**.

1 LITRE

This is the volume of food a stomach can generally hold.

YOU CAN PEE WITHOUT POOING, BUT YOU CAN'T POO WITHOUT PEEING

Have you ever noticed that when you sit down to do a poo you nearly always have a pee too, even if you didn't intend to? The way we poo and pee is controlled by round muscles called sphincters. The sphincter we use for peeing is smaller than the one we use for pooing, so when you pee you can relax it without relaxing all the muscles that support your bowels. This means you can pee without needing to poo at the same time. However, when you have a poo, the relaxation of the larger and stronger sphincter also relaxes the smaller sphincter and you find yourself having a pee too.

Unlike humans, birds do not have separate holes for their poo and pee. They pass a mix simultaneously through their cloaca. Next time you see a bird mess have a closer look. The white part is actually the bird pee and the dark centre is the poo.

Spring a leak

Of course, if you concentrate really hard you can hold your pee in while you have a poo. It is possible, but it's not advisable as if you do this repeatedly it can overstretch your bladder and lead to it becoming overactive and leaky.

7

This is the average number of pees people do in a single day.

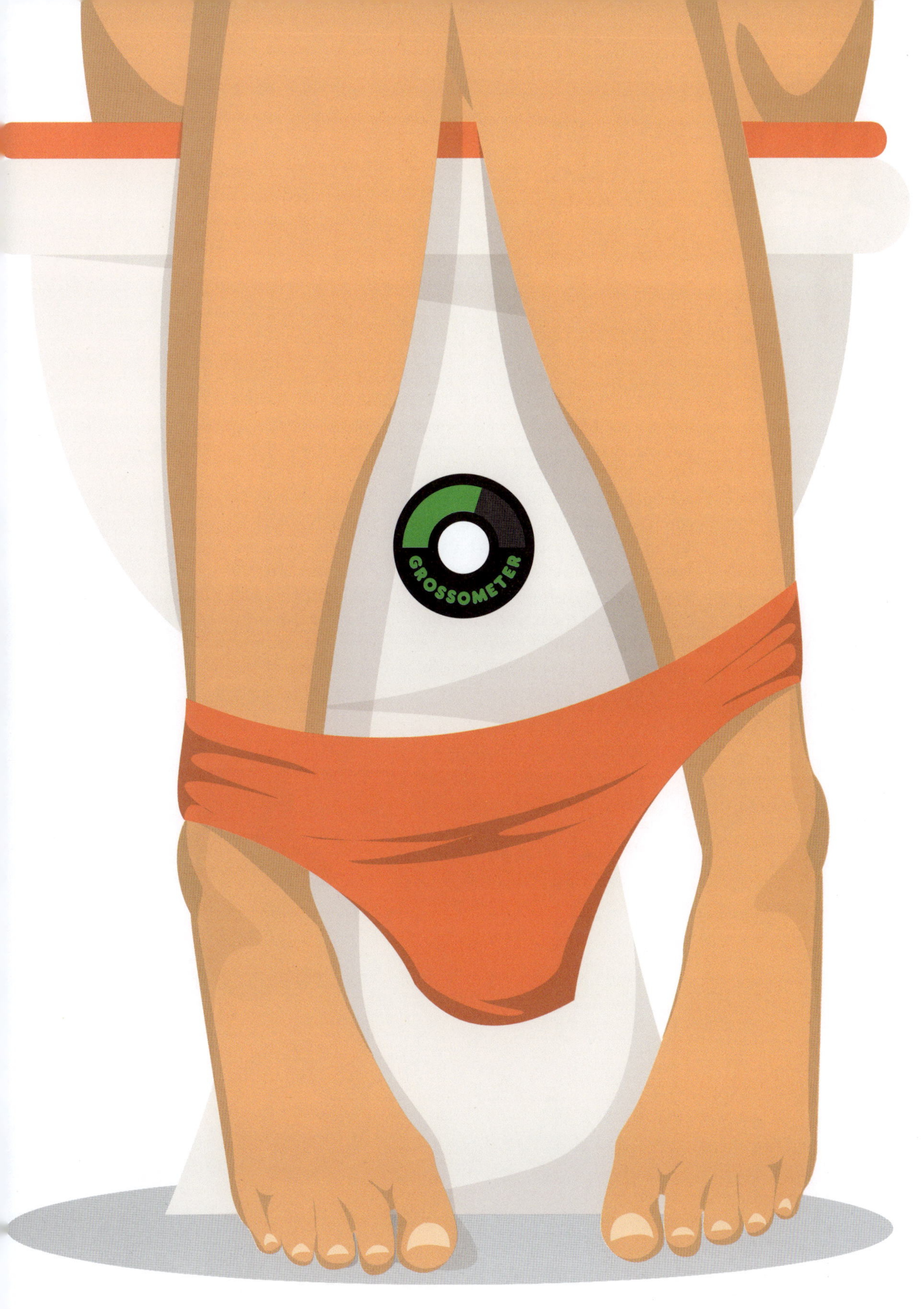
GROSSOMETER

MAKING A STRETCHY BLADDER

Pee is your body's way of removing waste and any water that it no longer needs. When you drink a lot of water your pee is nearly clear, and when you haven't drunk enough it's a darker yellow colour and a bit stinky. Your kidneys filter waste from your blood, and pee is how your body then removes the waste. Among other things, your pee contains water, salts, ammonia and urea (a waste product of proteins). The place where your pee is temporarily stored is called your **bladder**, a round bag-like organ that acts as a fleshy storage tank and is incredibly stretchy. As it fills with pee, your bladder goes from being the size of a pear into something that can hold roughly **half a litre** of pee. This experiment uses a balloon to show you just how much liquid half a litre is and how stretchy your bladder is to accommodate it.

Your body has sensors that can detect your bladder stretching. They send a signal to your brain telling you to go to the bathroom.

What you will need

500 millilitre measuring jug

Tap water

Balloon

Tap

How to stretch your bladder

1. Fill a measuring jug with half a litre of water from the tap, timing how long the tap is left on to do this.
2. Pour the water away and carefully stretch the mouth of the balloon over the tap.
3. Turn the tap on again for the same amount of time as last time, filling up the balloon.
4. Carefully remove the full balloon and note how much it has stretched and how heavy it feels. Just like your own bladder.
5. Pour the water into the measuring jug to check that it was roughly half a litre.

YOUR BRAIN FEELS LIKE A SOFT HEAVY JELLY

Right now, your brain is happily sitting inside your head, safely housed inside a bony covering called the **cranium**. The cranium protects your brain from injury because human brains are extremely fragile. They're sensitive and very easily deformed, not at all like the rubberised or preserved brains you may have seen in museums. They have a soft, squishy consistency, similar to a jelly, and they're probably heavier than you realise, with the average adult brain weighing around **1.4 kilograms**. That's a very heavy jelly.

Your brain is wrinkled because this makes it more efficient. Scientists believe that as we have evolved and our brains expanded, the folds were created to optimise how much brain matter can fit into our skulls. Your brain's pattern of wrinkles is unique to you, just like your fingerprints.

Floating

Your brain is basically just soft blobs of fat that could easily become deformed by the touch of a single finger. Brains are soft to the touch that for extra safety they float inside your skull in a bath of **cerebrospinal fluid** that prevents them from coming into any contact with bone.

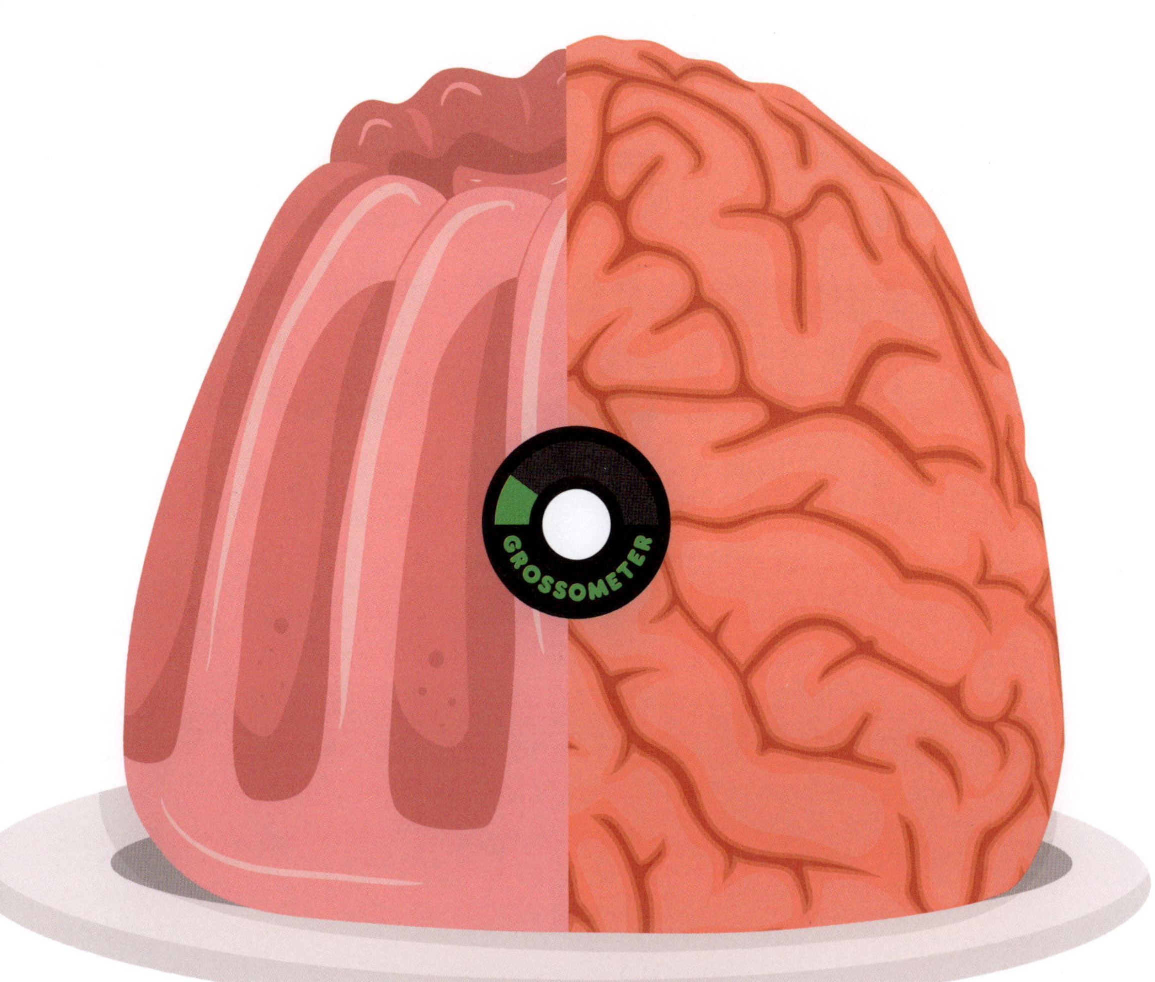

60%

This is the percentage of your brain that is made of **fat**, making it the fattiest organ in the body.

25%

This is the percentage of your body's total **cholesterol** that is found in your brain. Cholesterol is a fat that your body needs to work properly, but too much can cause health problems.

TO SURVIVE EXTREME COLD, YOUR BODY WILL SACRIFICE YOUR FINGERS AND TOES

At some point in your life, you've no doubt felt cold. Very cold perhaps. But you probably haven't been freezing. Well, not for long periods anyway. If you'd encountered extreme cold, your body would have done something extremely gross to keep you alive. In freezing temperatures, the blood flow to your fingers and toes stops in order to retain heat for the rest of your body. Your body does this without you knowing, which is probably for the best, because doing so causes these body parts to eventually blacken and drop off!

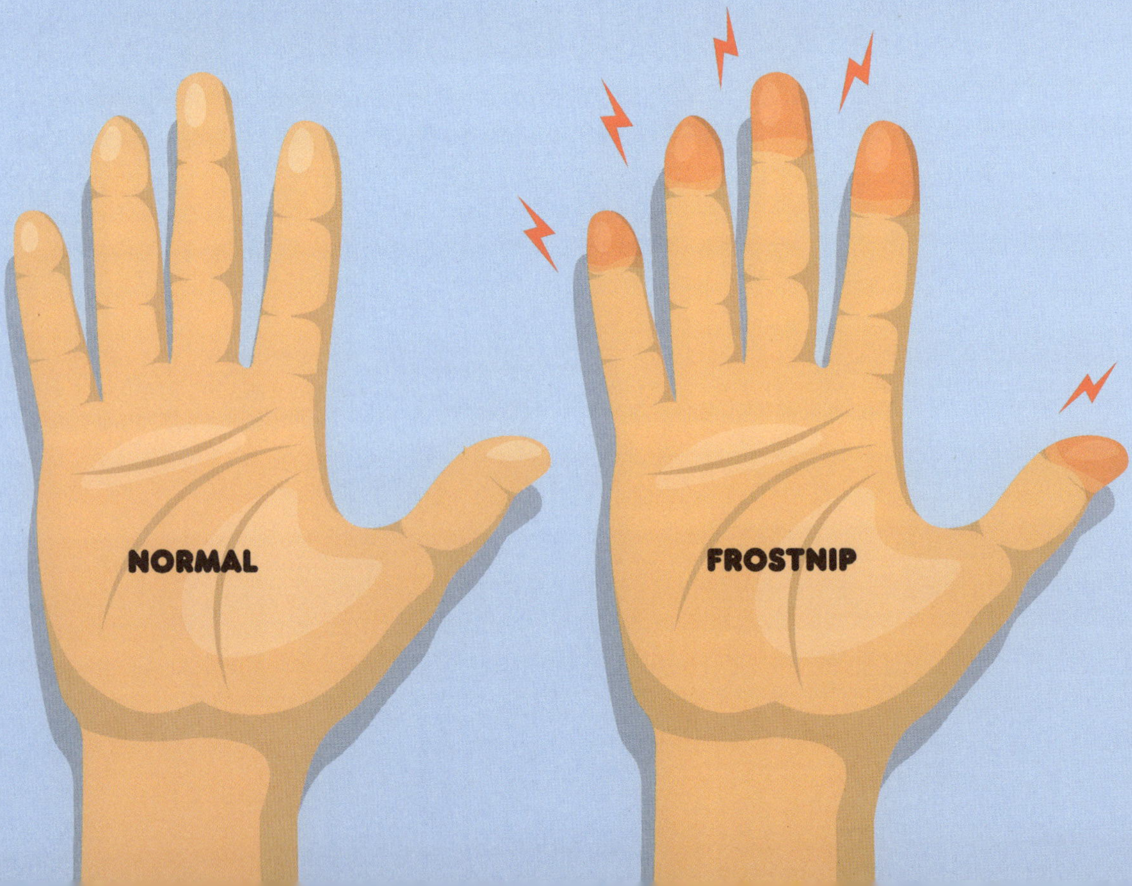

NORMAL

FROSTNIP

Drop off

The skin turning black is caused by ice crystals forming in the tissue because of the reduced blood flow to that area. The cells can die and that's when things start to drop off or have to be removed. This blistering and blackening condition is called **frostbite**.

Frostbite and heat burns are surprisingly similar injuries.

Cheeky

It isn't just toes and fingers that your body will sacrifice to keep you alive in very cold weather. People have lost **noses**, **ears**, **cheeks** and **chins**. Any part of the body that's frequently exposed to the cold and whose circulation is affected is at risk.

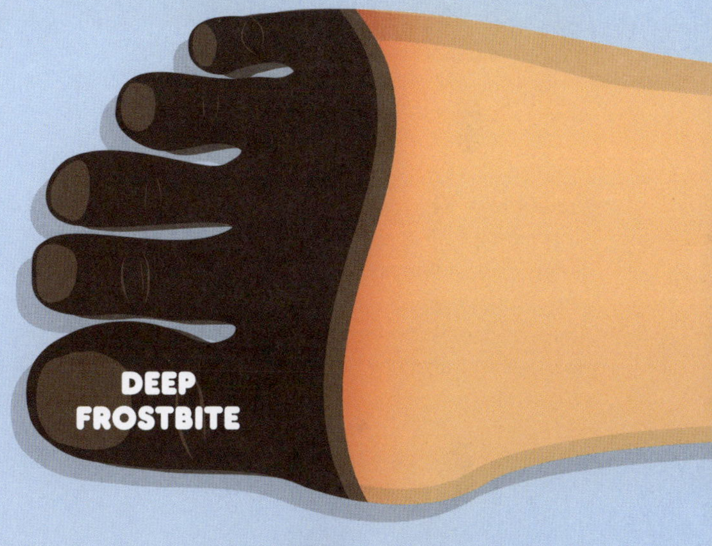

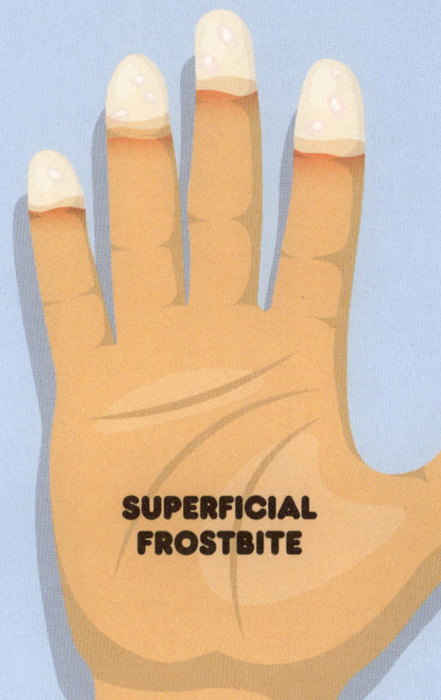

DEEP FROSTBITE

YOU PRODUCE MORE EARWAX WHEN YOU'RE STRESSED OR SCARED

Earwax may be gross, but that waxy oil produced by glands in your ear canals plays an important role. It protects and moisturises the skin of your ear canals, preventing dry and itchy ears. It also contains special chemicals that fight off potential ear infections, and it acts as a protective shield when dirt and dust enter your ear. But earwax has another role to that of protector: it can reveal your state of mental wellbeing. The stress hormone **cortisol** can be measured from the oily secretions around your ear canal. If you're feeling stressed or scared then your ear accelerates the production of more earwax. Exercise can also increase the amount too.

Fats cat

The medical name for earwax is **cerumen**. It contains oil and sweat mixed with dirt and dead skin cells. Absolutely revolting – but not if you're a cat, many of whom love to dine on the waxy secretions and receive nutrients and proteins from it.

Wet or dry

You can tell a lot about a person from their earwax. If it's wet, then they're probably Caucasian or African. If it's dry then they'll likely be Native American, Pacific Islander or Asian. If it's white and flaky then they'll lack the chemical associated with body odour.

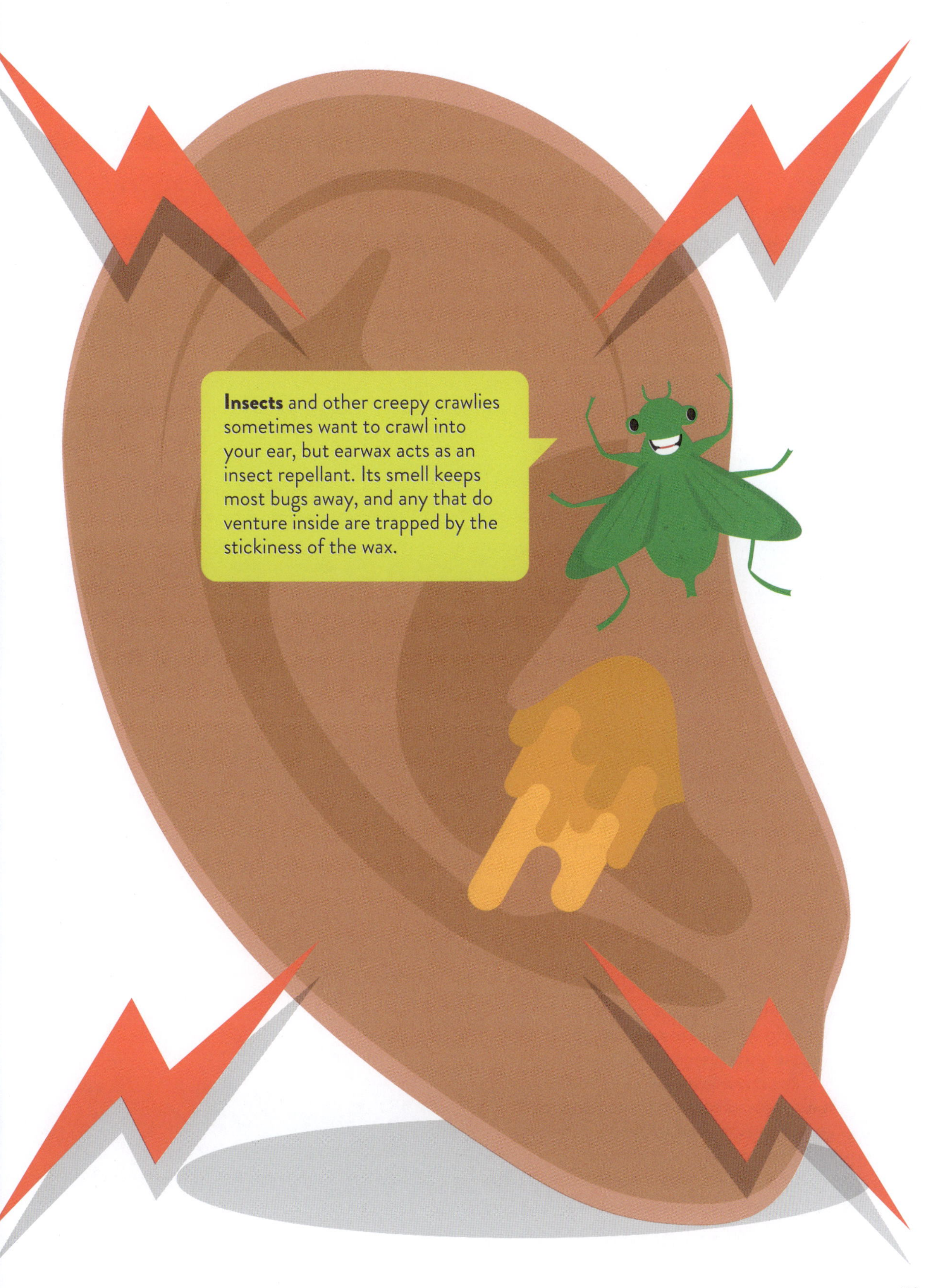

Insects and other creepy crawlies sometimes want to crawl into your ear, but earwax acts as an insect repellant. Its smell keeps most bugs away, and any that do venture inside are trapped by the stickiness of the wax.

YOUR BONES ARE WET

It's strange to think that there's a skeleton inside all of us. Skeletons are made up of **206** bones arranged in a particular way so that they hold us up and give us an internal framework. You'll have heard the expression 'dry as a bone' and have probably even seen and touched a bone, and felt how hard and dry it is.

But the truth is the exact opposite. When inside your body, your bones feel **wet** and a little **soft**. They are actually complex living organisms, producing blood cells, storing minerals, building muscles and communicating with other organs in your body. Bones are amazing, even if they are gross.

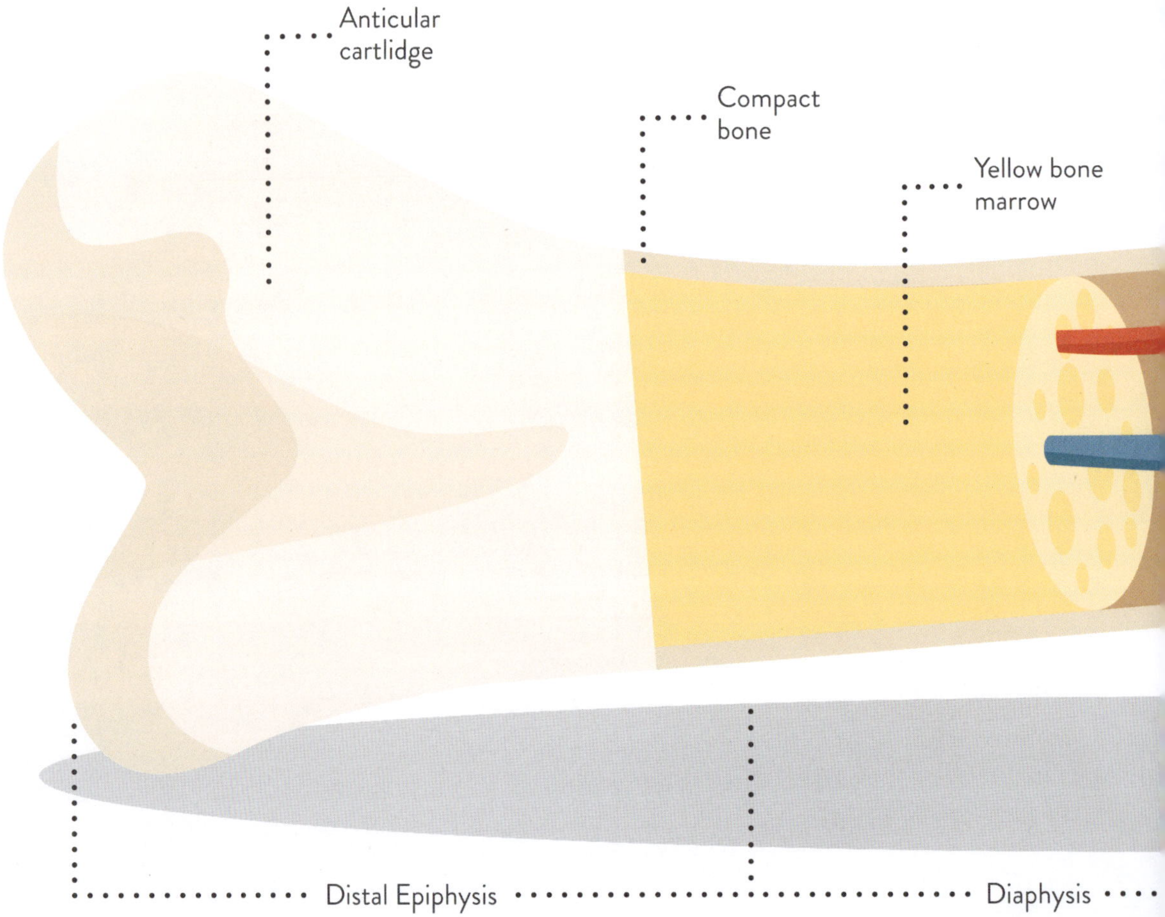

Anticular cartlidge

Compact bone

Yellow bone marrow

Distal Epiphysis

Diaphysis

A rush of blood

Like most parts of your body, bones have a network of blood vessels and nerves that run through them. If you break one of your bones it will bleed, and just like your skin they can get bruised.

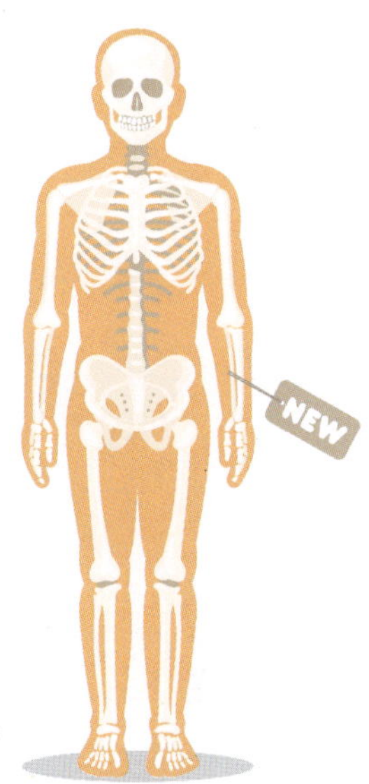

Short fuse

You actually have about **300** bones when you're born, but as an adult you end up with **206**. The reason for this is that lots of your bones fuse together as you grow.

Just like new

Bone is a living tissue and the collagen inside it is being constantly replenished. This means that about every **7 years**, you have a brand-new skeleton.

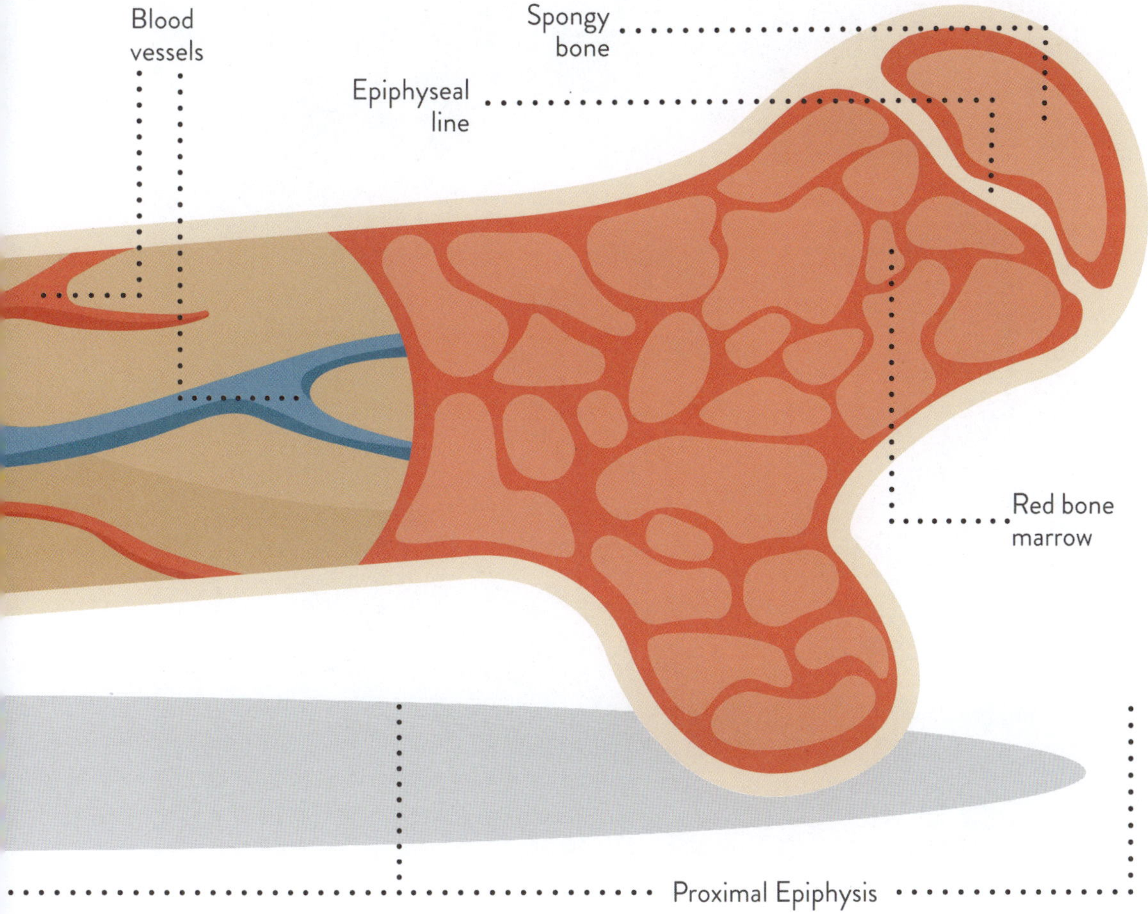

Blood vessels

Spongy bone

Epiphyseal line

Red bone marrow

Proximal Epiphysis

FOR SOME PEOPLE, THEIR EYEBALLS ARE NOISY

Imagine if you could hear your eyeballs moving in their sockets, and every time you looked up, down, left or right, there was a grating sound to accompany the movement. Like sandpaper. And it was a sound that only you could hear. Well, for a small number of people, this is an uncomfortable daily reality. It's due to a condition called **superior canal dehiscence syndrome** (SCDS). This condition is caused by a small hole in the bone covering part of the inner ear and results in distortion of hearing and impaired balance.

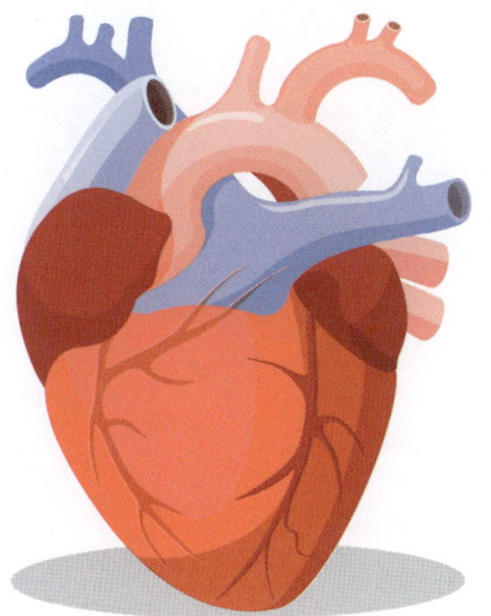

No laughing matter

In some cases of SCDS, the sufferers will fall to the ground whenever they burst out laughing, or loud noises cause them to feel dizzy and their vision can pulsate to the rhythm of their own speech. Even a cough or a sneeze can trigger the symptoms.

In a heartbeat

Sufferers from SCDS not only hear their eyeballs move in their sockets but can also sometimes hear their own heart beating and their pulse pounding. The interior sounds of their body are all heard particularly loudly.

Perpetual motion

If SCDS wasn't strange enough, another symptom is a feeling that things are moving when they aren't. This is called **oscillopsia**. It feels like the surrounding environment is in constant motion when it is, in fact, stationary.

TUMOURS CAN GROW EYES AND TEETH

Tumours are lumps in or on your body that shouldn't be there. They are from a new or abnormal growth of tissue, and they can be harmless, in which case they are called benign, or they can be cancerous, in which case they are called malignant. There's a type of tumour that's called a teratoma that has been known to sprout teeth and eyes, which would explain why its name translates roughly as 'monstrous tumour' in Greek.

Feeling nervous

As if having teeth and eyes wasn't disgusting enough, some teratomas have been known to contain all different kinds of tissue, bone, muscle, hair, and even elements of a nervous system.

In one case, a young girl was found to have a teratoma that contained the beginning of a brain and brain stem in a skull. All inside a tumour in her ovary!

Stem the tide

Even though teratomas look horrifying, they are mostly benign. By examining them, scientists made the discovery of **stem cells**, which might one day allow us to grow human organs in laboratories to help people who need transplants.

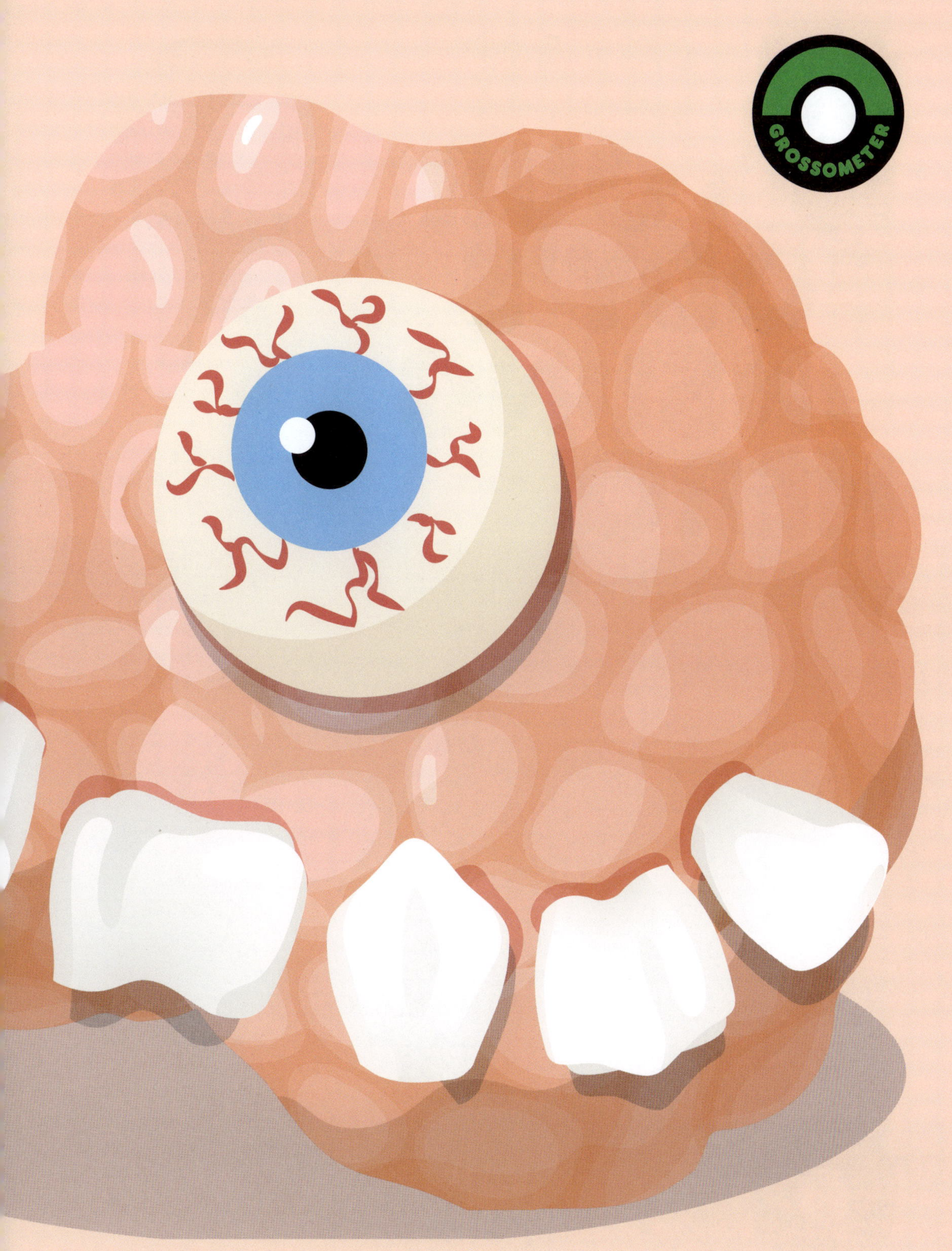
GROSSOMETER

MUCUS IS YOUR BODY'S UNSUNG HERO

Normally with mucus, you blow it into a tissue, or cough it up, then dispose of it as quickly as you can. Get it out and get it away! But mucus deserves a bit more respect because that stringy slime is your body's unsung hero and has a powerful affect on your health. It coats the surfaces of your guts, eyes, mouth, nasal cavity and ears. It also helps in hydrating and cleaning, helping good microbes and repelling potential invaders. Without that gross goop you wouldn't be alive!

Boogie down

Most of the mucus in your nose gets swept to the back of your throat. But sometimes, especially in dry conditions, some of the mucus near your nostrils begins to dry out. If it stays there for long enough it becomes a crusty booger.

If you ever pick boogers out of your nose you're in good company. Over **90 percent** of people admitted to doing this when questioned.

Put your coat on

Mucus coats the tissue lining of all your internal organs and cavities.

Eyes
Nose
Ears
Oral cavity

Respiratory tract
Liver
Gall bladder
Bile ducts
Pancreas
Gastrointestinal tract

Reproductive tract

1.5 LITRES

This is the average amount of mucus produced in **one day**. You swallow it without even noticing. You swallow, on average, **twice every minute**, even when you're asleep. I bet you've swallowed just now!

EXAMINING YOUR MUCUS

Next time you blow your nose or cough up some phlegm, don't dispose of it immediately. If you take a closer look at it and examine what colour it is, you can learn a lot about your current state of health. Be sure to wash your hands thoroughly afterwards.

Mucus, in its natural state, is **clear**. This means you are **healthy**. If you have congestion or a runny nose with clear mucus, you may have allergies.

Yellow mucus is an indication that there is an **infection** in your body, but don't panic just yet! This is exactly what should be happening as your body fights the infection.

Mucus with shades of **green**, especially darker shades, means you have an infection and your body is working super hard to fight it. It could be a sign of a more **serious infection**.

RED

Red mucus looks alarming, but usually just means your nasal passages are **dry** or **injured**. The red colour is a result of bleeding in your nasal cavity.

BROWN

Mucus that is **brown** could be because you inhaled something, such as **dust** or **dirt**. It can also be from dried **blood** in the nasal passages.

Black mucus may be a sign of a **fungal infection**. It might also be from inhaling **ash**, **dirt**, **dust**, **smoke** or similar substances in **air pollution**.

FOOD GORG

The world of competitive food-eating is a very strange one. And an extremely gross one too. People set out to eat as much of a particular food as they can in a set time period and the person who manages to cram the most down their throats is declared the winner. There's currently one man who is head and shoulders above everyone else: American **Joey Chestnut** is the greatest eater in history and has at one time held **55** world records to back this title up. Here are some of his revolting records.

GROSSOMETER

The number of **Big Macs** eaten in **38 minutes**.

The number of **mini glazed doughnuts** eaten in **5 minutes**.

The number of **hard-boiled** eggs eaten in **10 minutes**.

The number of **ice cream sandwiches** eaten in **6 minutes**.

ING FRENZY

The number of **hot dogs** eaten in **10 minutes**.

The number of **gyoza** eaten in **10 minutes**.

The number of **chicken wings** eaten in **30 minutes**.

The number of **Taco Bell soft shell beef tacos** eaten in **10 minutes**.

MAKING A DIGESTION BAG

Disgusting food habits aside, the real purpose of eating is to digest food so that our bodies can receive the vitamins, minerals and other essential nutrients from it. Digestion begins when we use our teeth to chew food and break it down into smaller pieces (**mechanical digestion**). The saliva in our mouths causes a chemical reaction that begins to digest the food before we swallow it. Our stomachs have proteins called enzymes that change the food into smaller molecules which our bodies can use (**chemical digestion**). Our blood then carries these smaller molecules all around our bodies and any waste is removed by going to the toilet. This simple experiment replicates the digestion process using crackers and soda.

What you will need

2 crackers

Plastic zip lock bag

3 tablespoons soda

How to make the digestion bag

1. Put the crackers in the zip lock bag.
2. Break the crackers up into smaller pieces to represent mechanical digestion, or chewing.
3. Add the soda to the bag. The soda contains acid, just like your stomach (chemical digestion).
4. Observe how the food now becomes a disgusting slurry. In our bodies, it's now ready to be passed on to our intestines.

ANI

ALS

FIGS HAVE DEAD WASPS INSIDE THEM

Have you ever eaten a **wasp**? Well, if you've ever eaten a **fig** then you probably have. What?! The answer lies with mother nature. Unlike apples and peaches, figs bloom inside their pear-shaped pods and their reproductive parts are located inside too. So, to become pollinated, the fig relies on a friend: the tiny female fig wasp. She enters the unripe fig carrying pollen and lays her eggs. She then rolls over and dies. But before you get too grossed out about all the times you've eaten a fig, don't worry – those crunchy bits are fig seeds, not wasp skeletons. Using enzymes, the fig digests the tiny insect and turns it into protein, which then becomes part of the flavour of the now ripened fruit.

Tunnel vision

When the baby wasps hatch inside the fig, they all mate and the wingless males chew a tunnel out of the fig before they too die. The females use this tunnel to enter the world for the first time. The cycle continues as they are now carrying fig pollen and are free to search for another fig tree where they can lay their own eggs

Lose your head

When the female wasp enters the fig, her wings and antennae are stripped away, and she becomes trapped. The wasps sometimes fight inside the fig if more than one enters, and lethal battles take place often involving decapitation!

900

This is the number of fig wasps responsible for pollinating the world's **900** species of fig. Each species of wasp only pollinates a specific species of fig. The fig attracts its partner wasp with a unique scent.

JELLY BEANS ARE MADE WITH INSECT POO

Jelly beans are great. Not only do they taste yummy but they also look brilliant too – so colourful and so shiny. But did you ever wonder why they are so shiny? And so hard too? The deceptively disgusting answer is because of insect poo, or Shellac to give it its proper title. In Thailand and India, the sticky resin secreted from the **Lac Bug** is scraped from the tree bark where they live and collected. It then goes through a heating process, after which it is cooled down, ready to be used as a confectioner's glaze in the manufacture of jelly beans.

Wax on

It's not only jelly beans that Shellac is used for. It's also applied to other candy, chewing gum and ice cream cones. It doesn't dissolve in water so prevents products getting wet or drying out. Fruits like apples, oranges and avocados are sometimes given a waxy coating with it.

Eating bug secretions may seem gross but it isn't that unusual. We get the food colouring Cochineal extract from dried insects similar to the **Lac Bug**. And perhaps most famously we eat honey, which after all is something that bees secrete. And it's delicious!

BEAVERS' BUMS HELP MAKE VANILLA ICE CREAM

GROSSOMETER

The next time you're enjoying a delicious vanilla ice cream, or indeed any food item flavoured with vanilla, you might want to think twice about just where that fantastic taste has come from. The 'natural flavouring' **castoreum** is sometimes used to flavour vanilla dairy products and desserts. Doesn't sound so bad, does it? Except Castoreum is a thick goo secreted from beavers' anal glands.

Mix it up

The beaver's castor sacs, which are found between its pelvis and the base of its tail, provide the fragrant chemical compound. Because of how close the sacs are to the anal glands, the gloopy goo is often a mixture of castor gland secretions, anal gland secretions and urine. What a combination!

Head on down

If you lift up a beaver's tail, get your head down there and stick your nose near its bum, you will smell a musky, vanilla scent. This is because of the beaver's unique diet of leaves and bark.

Castoreum consumption is rather small, only **132 kilograms** a year globally. Thankfully!

Little squirt

The beavers are 'milked' to extract enough **castoreum** for food production. The animal is sedated, and the sticky stuff is very carefully squirted out.

PARASITIC WORMS TURN SNAILS INTO DISCO ZOMBIES

Zombies are real and they're out there in nature. But rather than being animated human corpses wandering the streets looking to eat brains, these zombies are snails, and they appear to be having some kind of disco. The story of how these zombie snails are formed is more fascinating than any horror film too and involves a parasitic worm called **Leucochloridium**. This worm needs a host body to live in and take control of, and that body is a snail.

Bird brain

Once the worm has taken over the snail, its colourful larvae (baby worms) make their way to the snail's head and eyestalks and then wriggle around to look like a caterpillar. This is called 'aggressive mimicry'. In this case, they mimick a caterpillar, which means it's dinner time for any passing birds who spot them.

Higher ground

The snail starts to lose its sight due to infection and the worm then takes control over the snail, including its brain. To increase the chance of a bird seeing the amazing colourful show of mimicry, the worm directs the blind snail to higher ground or a well-lit area so that the larvae will be spotted and eaten by the bird.

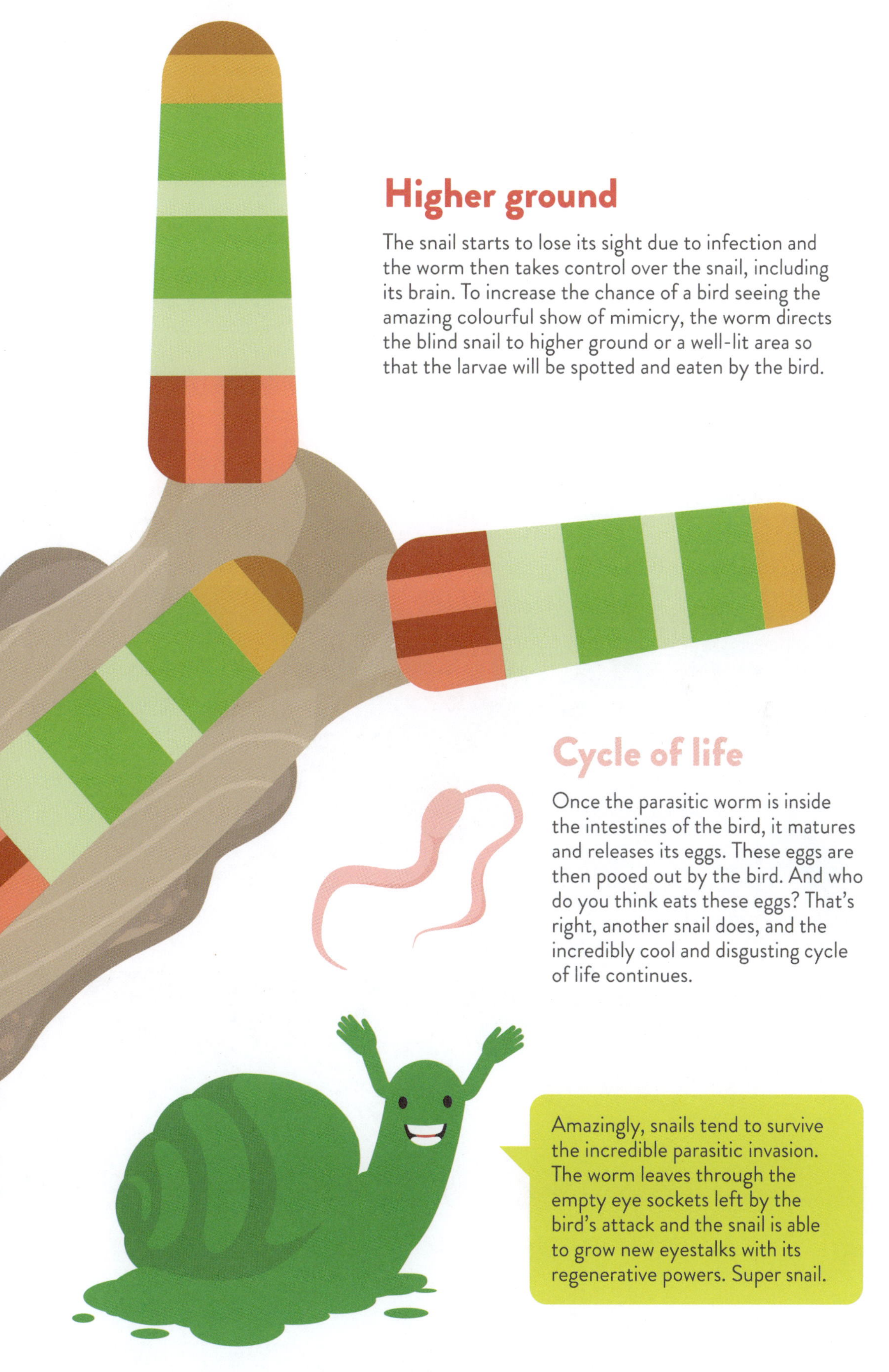

Cycle of life

Once the parasitic worm is inside the intestines of the bird, it matures and releases its eggs. These eggs are then pooed out by the bird. And who do you think eats these eggs? That's right, another snail does, and the incredibly cool and disgusting cycle of life continues.

Amazingly, snails tend to survive the incredible parasitic invasion. The worm leaves through the empty eye sockets left by the bird's attack and the snail is able to grow new eyestalks with its regenerative powers. Super snail.

THE HEAD-STACKING CATERPILLAR

The caterpillar of the **Uraba lugens** moth is just like all caterpillars: it must regularly shed its exoskeleton for it to grow. But unlike other larvae, this furry fella keeps its empty skull casings and stacks them on top of its noggin to form a bizarre and grotesque 'hat'. Anchored by sticky hairs, the caterpillar uses its revolting new headgear to confuse potential predators or swat smaller pests away.

The caterpillar is native to Australia and New Zealand, where it's earned the nickname 'The Mad Hatterpillar', after The Mad Hatter from Lewis Carroll's *Alice's Adventures in Wonderland*.

GROSSOMETER

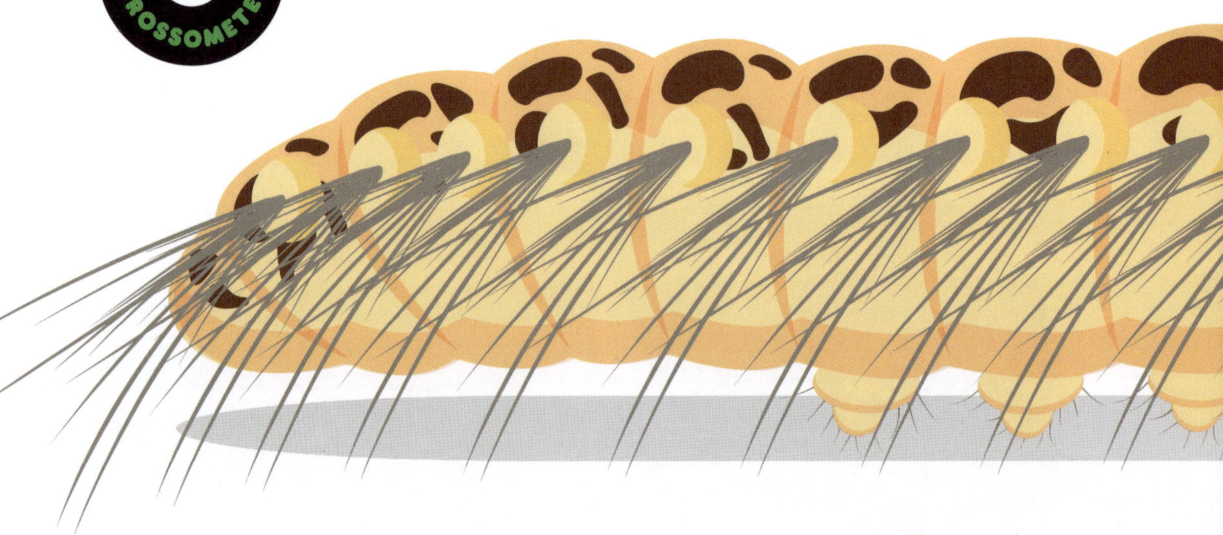

Bird poo

To avoid being eaten by birds, the **Viceroy** caterpillar has come up with an inventive way to protect itself. This clever caterpillar copies the colour of bird poo. They also behave like bird poo by hanging out on the underside of leaves.

Poo shoot

Because there are predators that are attracted to the smell of a caterpillar's poo, some caterpillars shoot poo pellets out their bums as far away from them as possible. **Silver-spotted skipper** caterpillars can throw poo pellets up to **1.4 meters** away from their nests, which is more than **40 times** their body length.

BUTTERFLIES EAT POO AND DRINK TEARS

Watching a beautiful butterfly fluttering its wings and floating delicately around the garden is like seeing a fairy in real life. But there's a darker side to these silky-souled creatures. They might drink nectar from flowers, but there are more revolting items on some butterflies' lunch lists. They eat poo and decaying flesh and will happily drink other animals' pee. They also drink the tears of turtles to gain the sodium and other minerals they need. This is a phenomenon called **lachryphagy**, which means 'tear-feeding'.

Mud puddling

Butterflies don't just love tears; they love poo too! It's a common sight to see a butterfly dining on a big sloppy pile of dung. It's called '**mud-puddling**' and it allows the butterflies to get the salts and amino acids they can't get from plants.

Pleased to meat you

Caterpillars are widely known as herbivores, capable of turning lush green leaves into mere skeletons in not much time at all. But for the **harvester** caterpillar of North America, meat is on the menu. This caterpillar lays its eggs on woolly aphids and the young caterpillars grow up eating the insects. For extra grossness, they will sometimes protect themselves with the corpses of their aphid victims.

A matter of taste

Butterflies will taste their food before they decide whether to suck it up through their mouthparts, which act as a straw. But unlike us, they don't have any tastebuds in their mouths. Instead, they taste food using their feet! As soon as they land on a plant, they can detect whether it is sweet, bitter, sour or salty.

MAKING A MUD PUDDLE TO ATTRACT BUTTERFLIES

As well as eating poo and drinking reptile tears, butterflies also pollinate flowers and add a dreamy quality to any garden that they flutter around. They drop in and out whenever it suits them, but there's a very simple way to attract them to your garden if you wish to.

What you will need

Soil

Water

Shallow dish or tray

Sunshine

Butterflies are attracted to **human skin** and they suck **sweat** and even **blood** from cuts with their proboscises. They also love **damp, sweaty socks** and **shoes**. What are they like!

How to make the mud puddle

1. Mix some soil and water in the shallow dish or tray to make a mud puddle.
2. Place the dish/tray in a sunny spot in the garden as butterflies rarely linger in shade.
3. Wait patiently for your fluttering friends to make an appearance.
4. Watch how the butterfly tastes with its feet first and then sucks up the water through its proboscis.

WOODPECKERS' TONGUES WRAP AROUND THEIR BRAINS

Your tongue flops around happily inside your mouth. For woodpeckers, though, it's a different story. Their tongues are so long that they wrap around the space between the woodpecker's skull and their skin, all the way around the back of their brain. This helps protect the brain from injury during all the high-velocity pecking they do.

Sharp or sticky

Woodpeckers have **sticky tongues** that are sometimes barbed. This helps to keep a hold of their prey. Just like a chameleon, they are able to launch and then pull in their tongues at an incredible speed.

Brain cooling

A woodpecker's head is designed in such a way that almost all the strain of pecking at a furious pace is transferred down its body. What small amount of force that is left is converted to heat in its head, which means that the bird must take breaks to let its brain cool down.

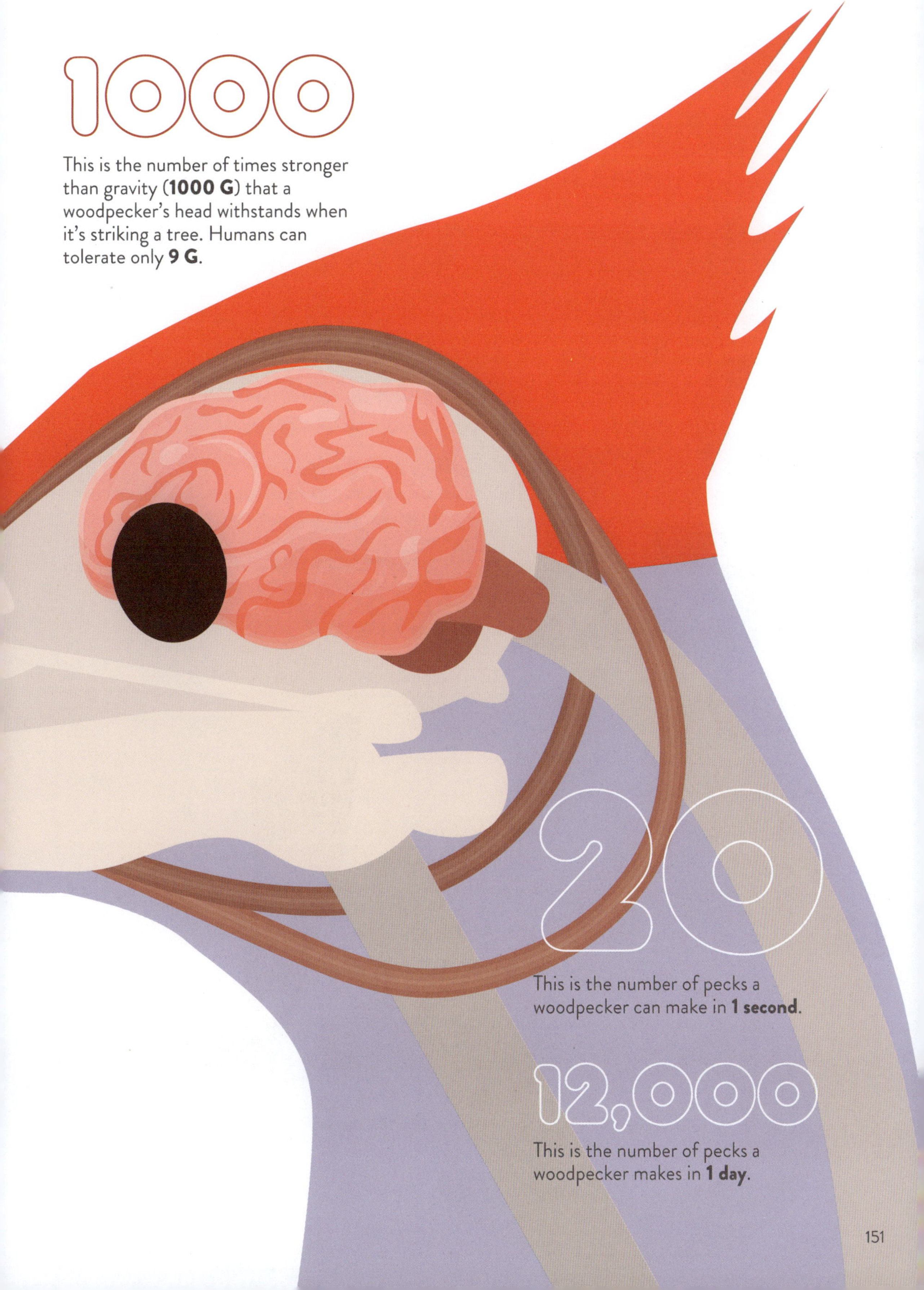

1000

This is the number of times stronger than gravity (**1000 G**) that a woodpecker's head withstands when it's striking a tree. Humans can tolerate only **9 G**.

20

This is the number of pecks a woodpecker can make in **1 second**.

12,000

This is the number of pecks a woodpecker makes in **1 day**.

CATS EAT THEIR OWNERS

A decomposing body is gross, but to a domestic cat this could be dinnertime. As shocking as it sounds, there are instances where cats have eaten their deceased owners. It tends to happen if the cat has become locked in after their owner has passed away. The cat only waits a couple of days before it tucks in!

Eating out

There are cases of feral cats who have slipped into houses where someone has passed away to dine on the dead body.

Dirty washing

Cats are usually able to go to the toilet without having any poo stick to their bums or fur. But if there's anything stuck there, they simply wash it off with their tongues. You might want to remember this next time your cat licks your face.

Bum call

When a cat repeatedly shows you its bum, it might appear rude. But this is the way cats greet us. Cats communicate through body language – they want you to take a hello sniff!

GIRAFFES CLEAN THEIR NOSES AND EARS WITH THEIR TONGUES

Tongues are handy. Their main job is to help us eat, but they have other uses too. You can wriggle your tongue around and clean bits of stuck food from your teeth. You can lick your lips if they feel dry. But your tongue pales in comparison to a giraffe's! Their tongues are so long that they can use them to clean out their nostrils and their ears!

The front of a giraffe's tongue is black, blue or purple. Experts believe that giraffe's tongues are so dark because they are out of their mouths and exposed to the sunshine for such long periods, leaving them open to sunburn. The darker colour is a result of the extra **melanin** present, helping to prevent sun damage and protect the long-necked lickers.

Get a grip

Just like a monkey's tail, giraffes' tongues are **prehensile**. This means they have developed muscular control, which gives them the ability to grasp things with it. The prehensile tongue allows giraffes to grip and pull leaves into their mouths, much like a hand or an elephant's trunk.

12 HOURS

This is the amount of time a giraffe's tongue is out of its mouth to help it eat in an average day.

55 CENTIMETRES

This is the length a giraffe's tongue can be.

That's about the same as a newborn baby.

HORNED LIZ SQUIRT BLO

Imagine for a moment that whenever you felt threatened by something or someone your body's response was to project blood at high speed out of your eyes at whatever was making you feel that way. It sounds horrific, but that's exactly what the **greater short-horned lizard** does!

ARDS
OD

A rush of blood to the head

Despite being covered in horns, the lizards face many predators. Their last-resort defence mechanism is to inflate their bodies up to two times their normal size and then squirt blood missiles from the corners of their eyes. Take that!

2 METRES

This is the maximum distance the lizard can fire its bloody tears – an impressive feat considering that the lizards themselves are only between **6** and **15** centimetres in length.

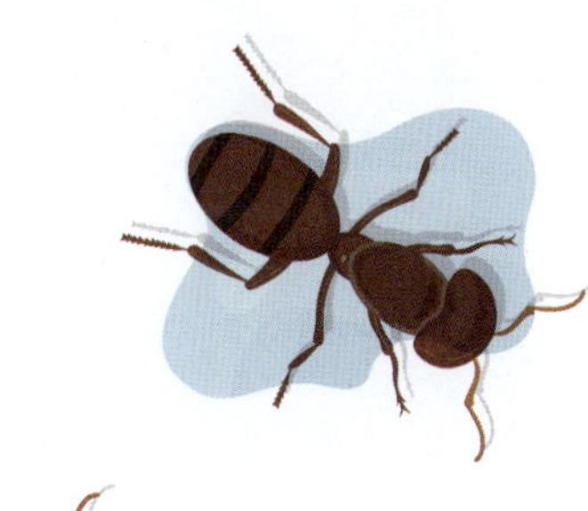

Slimeball

When the lizard isn't busy squirting its predators with blood, it becomes a predator itself. Its favourite food is ants, including the venomous ***harvester ant***. The lizard is clever, though – instead of crunching down on the ant and risking being stung, it catches the ant with its tongue, wraps it in slime and swallows it down whole. Gulp!

BUM-BREATHING TURTLES

Like a lot of animals, turtles go into hibernation during winter. They're cold-blooded, so as the temperature around them drops, so do their body temperature and metabolism rates. When **painted turtles** hibernate, they bypass their lungs and extract oxygen from the pond water around them through the surface of their bodies – in particular, their bums. They're bum-breathers! For these colourful little creatures, bum-breathing is the best source of oxygen when they go into pond hibernation during the cold months.

Mouth-watering

For the **soft-shelled turtle** in China, its cloaca isn't the only way it can pee. This unique creature also uses its mouth, which, rather strangely, helps keep it healthy and allows it to live in salty environments.

HIPPOS 'SWEAT' THEIR OWN SUNSCREEN

If you know it's going to be a hot day and you're going to be outdoors, then you slop on your sunscreen to save you from those damaging rays. But for a hippopotamus, that isn't a problem. All they need to do to create some protection from the sun is get sweaty. Their skin secretes an oily liquid that acts as sunscreen. It's colourless, but after a few minutes, turns pinkish red. It then mixes with their skin mucus and stays this colour for several hours before slowly turning brown over time.

Blood sweat

Originally this oily liquid was called **blood sweat**, but it doesn't contain blood. And it technically isn't sweat as it's produced by subdermal glands, not by sweat glands.

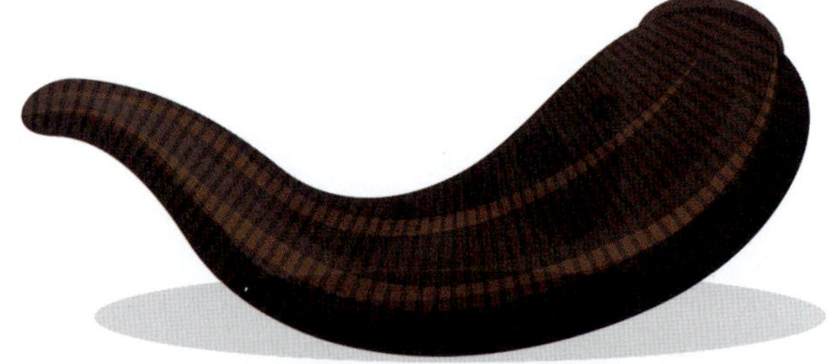

The acid test

Two pigments have been found in the oily secretion – **hipposudoric acid**, which is red, and **norhipposudoric acid**, which is orange. Both absorb ultraviolet light. As well as absorbing the light, the secretion also scatters it due to its crystalline structure, meaning it combines both sun-blocking and sun-screening properties.

Bum deal

Hippos' bums are home to one of nature's most disgusting stowaways – the **Placobdelloides**, or **Hippo Bum Leeches** as they're often called. These abominable blood-suckers clamp down and spend their lives latched onto hippos' bums where they happily feed away on blood vessels along the bum wall.

Tail spin

Hippos mark their territory using their poo. They spin their tails, which acts as a fan to fling their poo far and wide. Better watch out next time you're at the zoo!

SPIDER MUM MAKES A MEAL OF HERSELF

Becoming a mum is a beautiful thing: carrying the unborn child through pregnancy, giving birth and then nurturing and caring for the baby is one of life's joys. Mums would do anything for their kids. The female **Stegodyphus lineatus** spider takes mothering to a whole new level, though – she pukes up her intestines and lets her hungry kids gorge themselves silly on her digestive system. She literally feeds herself to her babies!

Melting moments

During her pregnancy, the spider mum's insides are already beginning to melt so that when her babies hatch, her liquefied organs will ooze out of her mouth, ready to be dined on by her new children. And this is how, over the next two weeks, the spider mum continues to feed her offspring, dissolving her internal organs one by one until her once enormous abdomen looks more like a shriveled-up balloon.

Bundle of joy

Every spring, the spider mum lays her eggs and then bundles them all up into a big sac. She carefully guards them from any passing male spiders, who would kill and eat them given half the chance. She fattens herself up by catching her own insect food as she watches her eggs.

Suck it up

With almost half her body now eaten, the spider mum finally dies, leaving her babies to fight over the rest of her corpse. They hungrily swarm over her body, piercing it and sucking out any remaining fluids.

TONGUE-STEALING FISH PARASITE

Parasites are nature's freeloaders and there are lots of different kinds. Some steal food that was gathered by another creature. Some force other animals to parent their children. Some use other creatures to get around. Some slowly destroy, suck the energy from or even take over the mind and behaviour of their unwitting host. The **Cymothoa exigua** is a unique type of parasite because once it's inside a fish, it eats a body part of its host and then becomes the replacement for that missing part. This is why the parasite goes by the name of 'the tongue-eating louse'.

Blood sucker

The way the isopod parasite eats the tongue is by sucking all the blood out of it until it just falls off. It then seizes this opportunity to grip the remaining stump and become the fish's brand-new parasitic tongue – whether the fish likes it or not.

Dinnertime

While impersonating the fish's tongue, the parasite will feed on the fish's blood and mucus. Delicious.

Get changed

The tongue-eating louse is female but was born male, as they all are. As a baby, the louse enters the fish through its gills and begins to mature, but once another young male arrives on the scene, the first one transforms into a female. This is when she decides to crawl into the fish's mouth and start sucking away at that yummy tongue.

CHICKENS EAT THEMSELVES

When you think about chickens you probably have an image of our feathered friends slowly walking around a coop, stopping continually to have a peck at some corn they've found on the floor. But this doesn't give you the whole picture. Chickens are **omnivores**, meaning they eat a variety of food of both plant and animal origin. They will basically eat anything. And I really do mean anything, including each other and even themselves!

Chicken dinner

Chickens are **cannibals**, which means they will eat some, or even all, of another chicken as food. They don't stalk and hunt one another around the farm, but under negative conditions, such as cramped living conditions and overcrowding, a flock can start picking and pecking at one another.

Chickens will continue to flap their wings and run around even after their heads have been chopped off. After finding themselves headless, they can still run the length of a football pitch. There was even a chicken called Miracle Mike who lived for **18 months** without a head.

Eat up

Where things get really gross is when a chicken starts to peck at itself. Again, the conditions must be very bad for this to happen, but chickens will peck away at themselves if they have an open wound. They have been known to eat away their own tails to the point where all that's left is a stump.

Egg on your face

If chickens are not satisfied by their diet, they have been known to eat their own raw eggs after laying them.

Pecking order

The phrase 'pecking order' comes from chickens. Bigger, stronger, more aggressive chickens bully their way to the top of the flock by pecking the others until they give in. This dictates who gets attacked and eaten. A lesser ranked bird with an open wound or an injury that bleeds can be an invitation to the rest of the flock to start attacking the poor victim.

Frenzied flock

As soon as chickens see blood, they go a little berserk. It sends the flock into a frenzy and they attack the wounded chicken. The more blood there is, the more the attack worsens. The crowd literally goes wild.

CAMEL PEE IS AS THICK AS SYRUP

Camels are legendary for their humps and their ability to endure long periods of time without food or water. They're less famous, however, for their thick, gross, gooey, gel-like pee – pee that's as thick as syrup.

Make a stink

Camel pee has a thick syrupy consistency because their kidneys are very good at absorbing and conserving water to help them survive the extreme desert conditions. Not only is their pee gooey, but it has a very strong smell and is super salty too.

Drink it down

People on the Arabian Peninsula have been drinking camel pee for a very long time, believing it to have medicinal health benefits. They've also used it as shampoo. Often it is mixed with camel milk and is said to taste absolutely disgusting.

Poo fuel

Much like their pee, people have found a use for camel's poo too. The small egg-sized pellets are so lacking in moisture that they can be burned without having to dry them out first. The poo is slow burning and virtually smokeless, making it perfect as a cooking fuel.

FROGS LIVE IN ELEPHANT POO

Frogs live in elephant poo. It may not smell the best or look beautiful, but when it comes to elephant poo, there really is no place like home for some species of **frog**. During the dry seasons, the frogs choose to cozy down in the poo of the **Asian elephant**. Though the reasons why are not clear, what is certain is that fresh elephant poo offers a cooler and more humid environment during the heat of the day. As well as providing shelter, there's always dinner on the table too, as elephants poorly digest their food leaving a lot of undigested, fibrous food for the frogs to feast on.

Sticky situation

Elephant poo has an extremely strong smell, similar to rotting fruit or vegetables. It's brown or black in colour and feels smooth and sticky if you touch it. As you would imagine, it's big too – about the size of a softball.

Good neighbours

The frogs are not alone in their poo paradise. Living alongside them are beetles, termites, ants, spiders, scorpions, centipedes and crickets. The poo serves as a self-containing ecosystem for all the creatures.

100 KILOGRAMS

This is the amount of poo an elephant can produce in a single day.

The same average weight as a giant panda bear.

GIANT LEECHES

Leeches are parasitic, oozing, gelatinous worms who attach themselves to their prey (including us) and then suck their blood. They often swell up to many times their original size as they gorge on their unsuspecting dinner. Pretty gross stuff. There are almost **700** different species of leech and on average they're around **50 mm** long, but there's one species that is monstrous in size. The **Haementeria ghilianii**, or **giant Amazon leech**, can grow up to **450 mm** in length. And with a proboscis that can be as long as **150 mm** it's able to drink a lot of blood too!

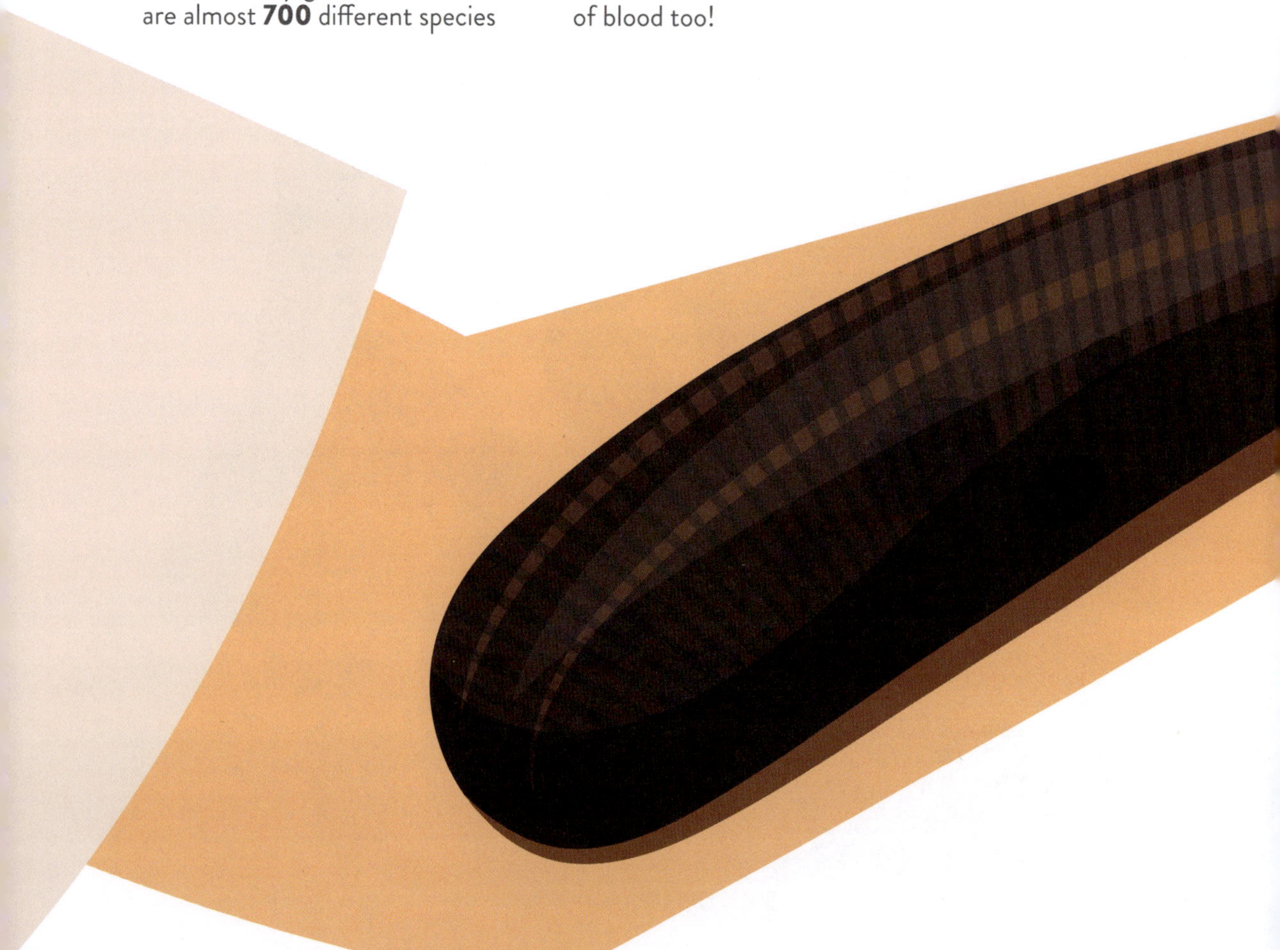

Feeling numb

Leeches can feed on their prey undetected because their saliva contains an anesthetic that numbs the skin and prevents their prey from even feeling the bite. The saliva also includes an anticoagulant that keeps the blood of their prey flowing when the leech bites.

Tyrant King

Most leeches are happy to feed on areas like the toes and necks of their prey, but the **tyrant king leech**, of the Amazon in Peru, focuses on very different human body parts. Anyone unfortunate enough to encounter this leech should beware – and not just because of its larger than average teeth and size. They should cover their eyes, bums and any other opening on their body as these leeches have a nasty habit of entering human bodies through these.

Not everyone thinks leeches are gross, slimy and horrifying. Some people love to keep them as pets and they even allow them to feed on their own blood.

GROSSOMETER

BABY KOALAS EAT THEIR MUM'S POO

Koalas aren't the first animal that springs to mind when you think about gross creatures. For one thing, they're incredibly cute and they have the most adorable babies, known as **joeys**, which they keep in their pouches. It's a very sweet sight. What is gross about these marsupials though is that at **6** months old, baby koalas eat their mum's poo. And not just any old poo – this is a special poo called '**pap**' and it's extra creamy and it's extra wet.

Soft and runny

The pap is soft and runny and comes from a pouch connected to the koala mum's intestines. It contains nutrients and gut bacteria that are vital to the joey's development.

Gets everywhere

When the joeys are feeding on the pap, they use their mouths to stimulate their mum's cloaca to produce their dinner. And because it's wet, it gets everywhere.

Koalas smell terrible – or at least the males do. Females and joeys smell similar to eucalyptus cough sweets, whereas the males have a more pungent pong.

FLIES VOMIT ON YOUR FOOD

GROSSOMETER

Unlike us, flies don't have any teeth, so when it comes to digesting food they do things a little bit differently. A hungry fly will land on its food and then vomit out a mixture of stomach acids and saliva. This liquid turns a solid meal into a soup, thanks to digestive enzymes that break down the food. Using its proboscis, the fly is then able to suck up its liquified dinner, which if it was your food the fly landed on, is your dinner too. Still hungry?

Pass it on

As well as vomiting on and liquifying your sandwiches, flies love nothing better than to dine on revolting things like poo and rotting meat. Often these are full of harmful bacteria that can be transferred to the fly when it lands. And then the fly can go and land on your food, passing the microbes on to you.

Flies can transmit over **65** different diseases to humans. These diseases include typhoid fever, cholera and tuberculosis. But if the fly doesn't stay longer than a few seconds, the chances of bacteria transferring is low, so your food should be okay.

Vomit bubble

Just like their unique way of digesting food, flies have an inventive way of fitting more in their stomachs too. They regurgitate food into vomit bubbles to dry it out a bit, reducing its liquid content. Then, once some water has evaporated, they ingest this more concentrated form of food.

Park and poo

Not only are flies vomiting on your food, but they're pooing on it too. Nearly every time a fly lands anywhere, it poos. This is because their liquid-only diet means food moves swiftly through their digestive system. And onto your sandwiches!

EAT LIKE A FLY

You're used to picking up food, putting it in your mouth and then chewing before you swallow it down. You do it every single day. So what would it be like if you ate like a fly? There's a simple way to find out. But don't worry – you don't have to vomit up saliva and stomach acids!

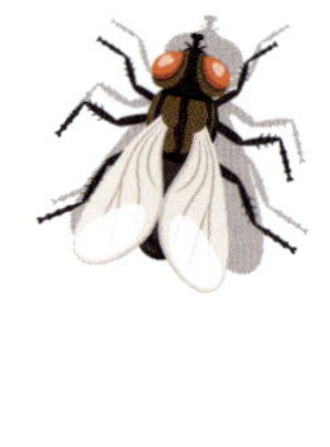

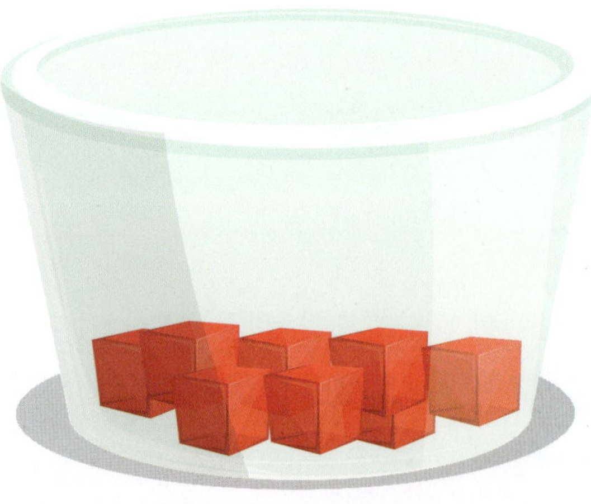

What you will need

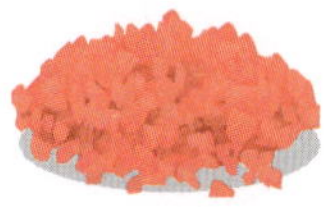

Jelly (made as per the packet instructions and cut into cubes)

Bowl

1–2 tablespoons white vinegar

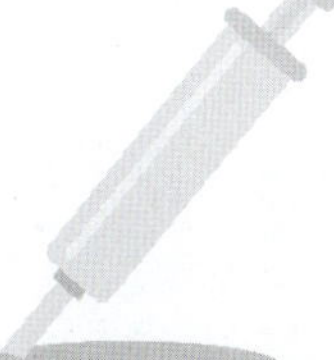

Syringe

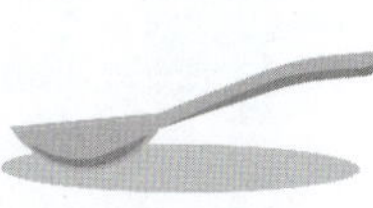

Spoon

How to eat like a fly

1. Place the jelly cubes in the bowl.
2. Pour the white vinegar onto the jelly to mimic the fly's vomit. Observe what happens.
3. Using the spoon stir the jelly lightly.
4. Use the syringe to mimic a proboscis and suck up the liquefied jelly mixture just like a fly.

SCIE

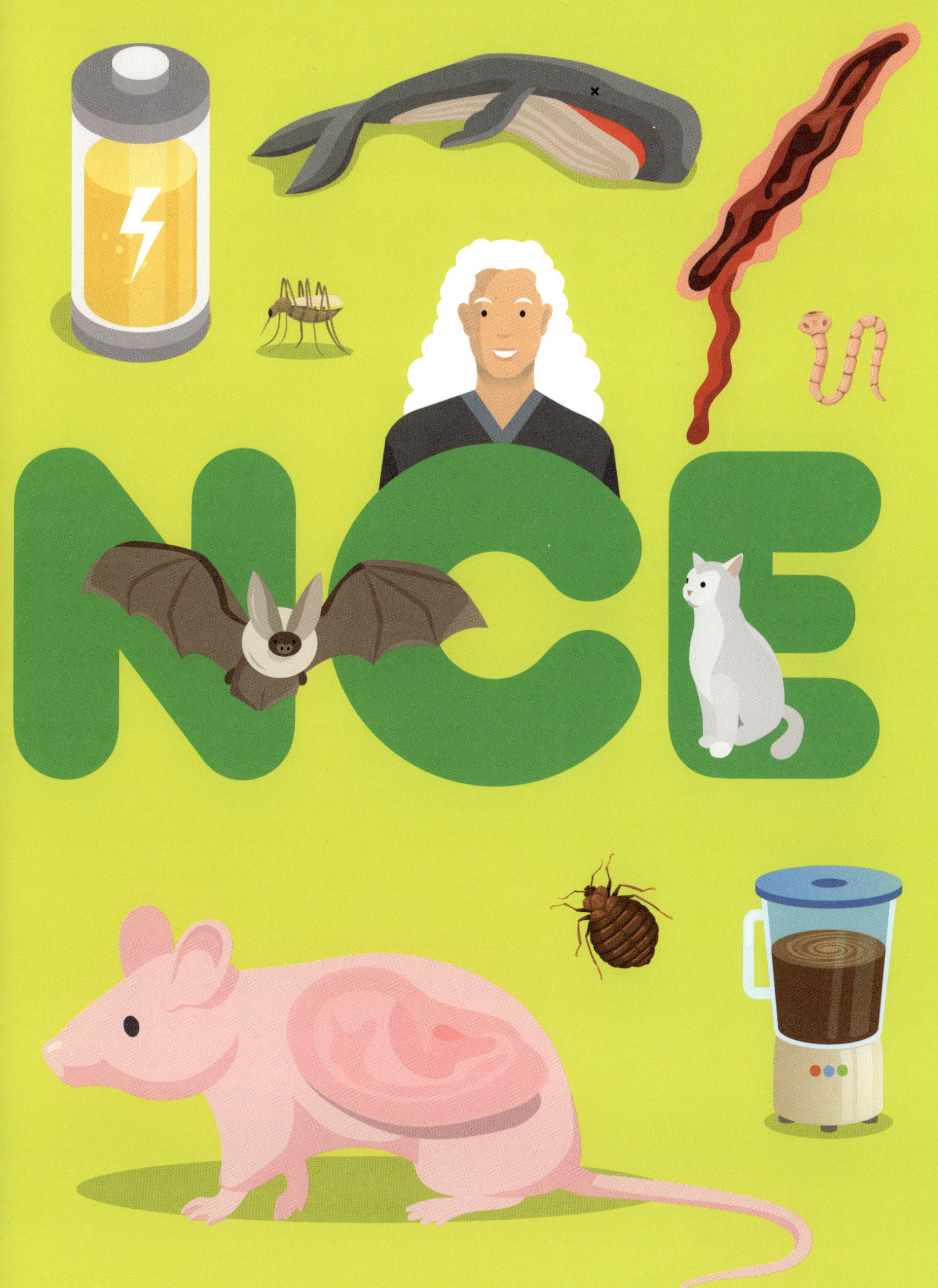
NCE

EINSTEIN'S EYES AND BRAIN WERE STOLEN

Albert Einstein transformed our understanding of the universe. The German-born scientist was one of the most important people of the 20th century. He was recognised numerous times for his contributions to science, and in 1921 was awarded the Nobel Prize in Physics. He was so famous, in fact, that when he died his brain was stolen after an illegal autopsy and remained missing for **50 years**.

Eye eye

Einstein's autopsy was carried out by Dr Thomas Stoltz Harvey, who removed the brain just **7 hours** after Einstein's death. The doctor stole his eyes too. The eyes are still kept in a security deposit box in New York to this day.

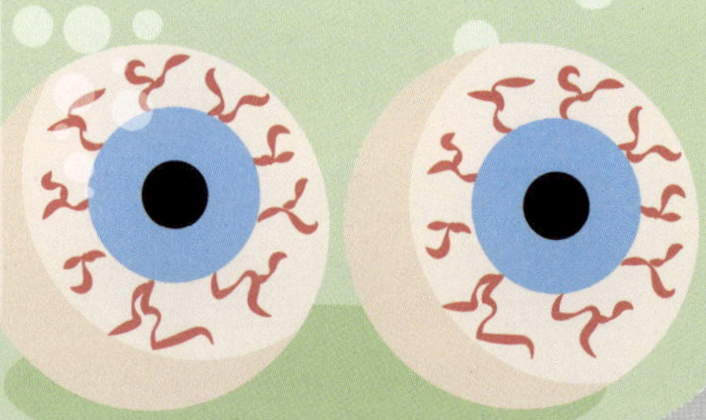

Heads up

The reason why Einstein's brain was stolen remains a mystery. The autopsy went against Einstein's direct wishes to be cremated with his brain still inside his head.

YOUR PEE GLOWS UNDER UV LIGHT

When you're dehydrated, your pee changes colour and becomes a much darker shade of yellow. It's a good reminder to drink more water. But that's not the only way your pee can look different. If you were to shine an ultraviolet light on it, it would glow. This is because pee contains phosphorus – an essential mineral in our bodies – and when phosphorus reacts with oxygen it glows. Pee also contains protein fragments, which react with the light.

Cats and dogs

It isn't just human pee that glows in ultraviolet light – most mammals, such as dogs and cats, will have glowing pee. Cat pee glows the most of all because it contains the most phosphorus.

508 SECONDS

This is the world record for the longest ever pee by a human. That's **8.5 minutes**!

Whiter than white

In ancient Rome, doctors advised their patients to wash their mouths out with pee for whiter teeth! Amazingly, this wasn't the world's worst idea as there's ammonia in urine which would make your teeth whiter. Don't try this at home though.

SCURVY CAUSES SCARS TO REOPEN

Scurvy isn't a disease you hear about much in modern times. It was common in the past where long-distance sailors would fall victim to it by not eating enough fresh fruit and vegetables. This left their bodies with dangerously low levels of **vitamin C**, resulting in bruising, weakness, anemia, gum disease, hemorrhage and loss of teeth.

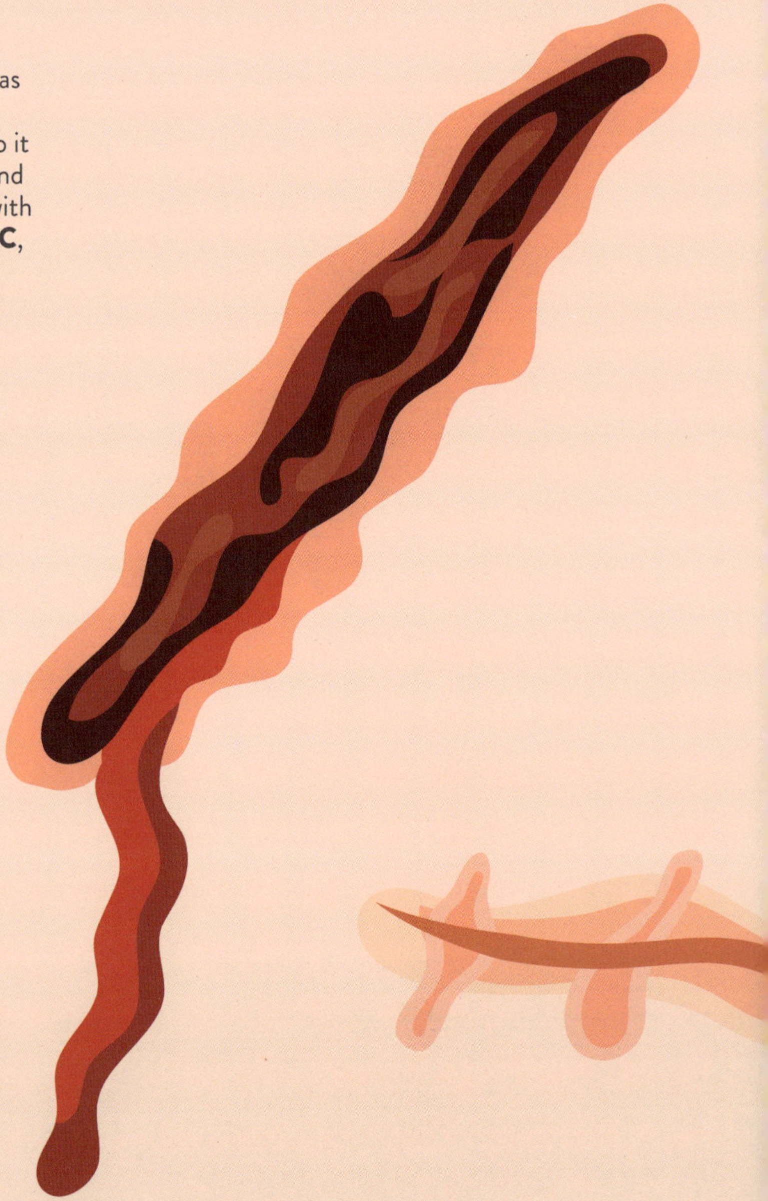

Break it up

Scurvy can cause a complete disintegration of the body. Skin begins to break apart and develop ulcers. Gums blacken and bones that had previously been broken and healed can re-break. Old wounds re-open too, including any scar tissue.

Rattle and creak

One of the major effects of scurvy is that the body can no longer produce collagen, which acts as a glue for the body's cells. This causes cartilage to disappear, meaning those with scurvy would rattle and creak when they moved around.

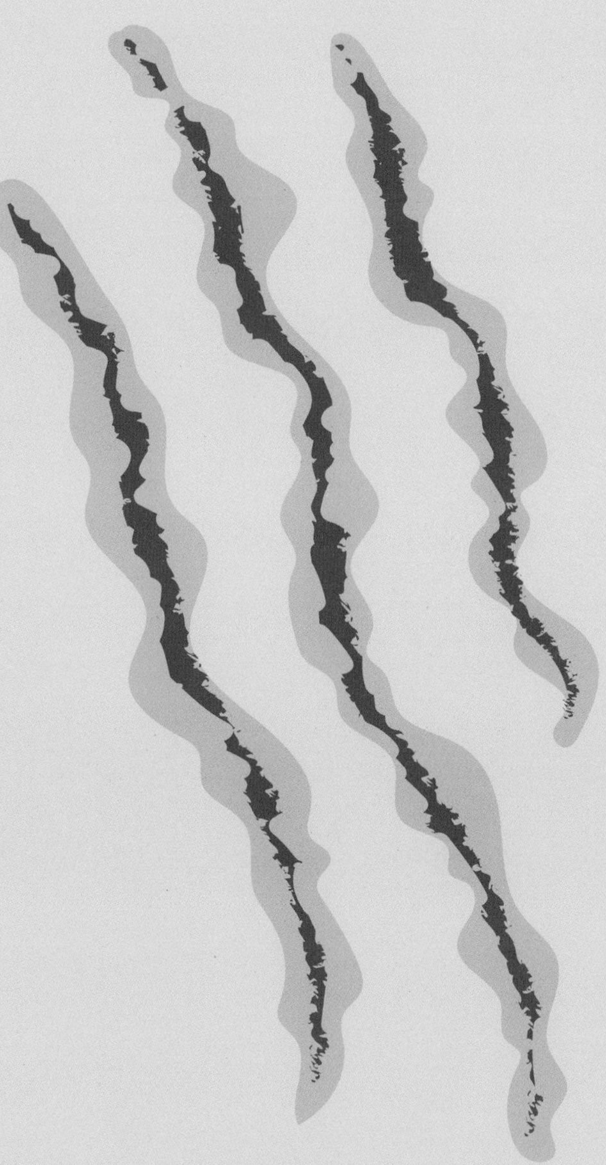

2 MILLION

This is the number of sailors who died from scurvy during the 'Age of Sail', a period from the **1490**s to the **1850**s.

Stick around

Although it was prevalent in the old world, scurvy does still exist today, even in some of the world's richest countries. And the reason is just the same as it was for those long-distance sailors from the past: not having enough vitamin C in your diet due to a lack of fresh fruit and vegetables. Homeless people and the elderly are especially prone to it. Better go eat some oranges!

SLIME CAN NAVIGATE A MAZE

If you've ever found yourself lost in a maze you'll know just how challenging it is to find your way out. But for **slime mould** this isn't a problem. These oily organisms can easily navigate a maze, finding the shortest route out as they do so. This is no mean feat considering they don't have a brain, but they can still somehow 'learn' as they go through the maze.

Vomit and poo

Some slime moulds form very odd shapes and have names that match, like 'dog vomit' and 'bird poo'.

Rotting logs

You may have seen these oozing globs of goo yourself. They really get around and are most commonly found on the floors of forests and on rotting logs. In urban areas, slime moulds can be found in garden mulches, gutters and even inside air-conditioning units.

MAKING SUPER SLIME

You know the type of super gooey slime you see in movies – the thick, gloopy, shiny kind that looks absolutely great? Well, how would you like to make some of that for yourself? It's really easy, and the slime is non-toxic, but it's very important to have parental supervision when you're making it and finding your ingredients. And remember to always wash your hands after playing with the super slime. Happy sliming!

Your slime will last longer if you seal it in a plastic bag and keep it in the fridge, otherwise it will dry out or go mouldy.

What you will need

- ½ cup polyvinyl alcohol (PVA)
- Beaker, jar or bowl
- Food coloring (optional)
- 2 teaspoons Borax (sodium tetraborate)

How to make the slime

1. Pour the polyvinyl alcohol (PVA) solution into a beaker, jar or bowl.
2. If you want coloured slime, add food colouring of your choice to the PVA solution and stir with a spoon.
3. Add the Borax into the PVA solution and stir slowly.
4. You have now made super slime and are free to have slimy, slimy fun with it. Just don't eat it!

SIR ISAAC NEWTON STUCK A NEEDLE IN HIS EYE

Sir Isaac Newton is widely regarded as one of the most influential scientists of all time. He was a mathematician, physicist, astronomer, alchemist, theologian and author. Famously, he discovered the mathematical principles that described everything from falling apples to orbiting moons, planets and comets. What he is less famous for is sticking a long sewing needle with a blunt point straight into his own eye socket!

Under pressure

The needle Newton inserted into his eye was called a Bodkin. Technically, he put the long needle into the area between his eye and the bone next to it as part of an investigation. He was examining vision and colour perception, and by sticking the needle in and applying pressure he could distort his eye. The result was that he saw several white, dark and coloured circles.

Behave yourself

Newton spent a lot of time in his laboratory working on all sorts of experiments. When some of his preserved hair was analysed, it was found to contain high levels of toxins such as mercury and arsenic. This has led some historians to believe this is what caused his behaviour, as he was famously highly irritable.

SCIENTISTS WHO EXPERIMENT ON THEMSELVES

Scientists take their work very seriously. And personally too, as sometimes they bravely experiment on themselves. History is full of men and women who have been their own test subjects to carry out their scientific enquiries. Steaming themselves in a vomit sauna? No problem. Injecting themselves with worms? Easy peasy. It's all in a day's work for these brave scientists.

Hook, line and sinker

Immunologist-biologist **David Pritchard** believed that certain parasites could improve the immune system in its defence against allergies and more serious autoimmune illnesses. Using himself as his first test subject, he injected **50 hookworms** under his skin. This led him to discover that only **10** hookworms were necessary for testing future subjects.

A bug's life

Biologist **Regine Gries** rolls up her sleeves every Saturday night and for **10 minutes** lets **1000** tiny, hungry, bloodsucking monsters dine on the flesh of her arms. The creatures are bedbugs and she does this in order to advance our knowledge and understanding of this invasive pest. She carefully keeps **5000** of them in her laboratory and has been bitten over **200,000** times in the name of science.

Vomit sauna

There was a time when **yellow fever** was one of the world's most feared human diseases. It was characterised by the disgusting black vomit of those infected with it. **Stubbins Ffirth** suspected that the viral disease was not, however, contagious and he tested on himself to prove this. He poured vomit into his open cuts and eyeballs, drank glasses of infected black vomit and even sat up to his waist in a sauna of vomit. After remaining free of the disease, he declared it non-contagious. He was half right, as later scientists discovered that it was contagious, but only through bites from infected mosquitos.

Tape it up

Giovanni Grassi was an Italian physician and zoologist who took his science to extreme measures. He believed that parasitic **tapeworms** could transfer from one host to another without any intermediary. And to prove this he extracted **100** tapeworm eggs from a dead man's poo and then ate them! About a month later, he was examining his own poo and when he discovered tapeworm eggs in it, he had the proof he required – as well as a new pet tapeworm living in his guts.

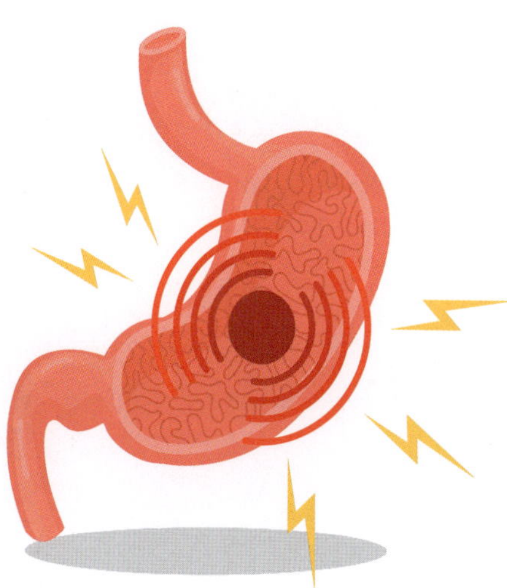

Stomach ache

When physician **Barry Marshall** first declared that he believed it was bacteria that caused stomach ulcers, rather than stress and spicy foods, he was mocked by other scientists. But he knew he was right and to prove this, he bravely drank a culture of the **H. pylori bacteria**, which, a week later, led to him developing terrible stomach pain and painful gastritis. He was indeed infected, but after a swift course of antibiotics, he was cured. This was such a breakthrough in science that he was awarded a Nobel Prize for his self-experimentation.

THE SCIENTIST WHO ATE EVERYTHING

William Buckland was one of Victorian England's leading geologists and paleontologists. His knowledge of the animal kingdom knew no bounds, and as President of the Royal Geographical Society he was the first scientist to publish a scientific study of a dinosaur skeleton. His role at the Society for the Acclimatisation of Animals allowed him to study all manner of creatures, to assess their suitability as food for UK dinner tables. His lifelong ambition was to eat a sample of every single animal in existence.

As quiet as a mouse

From porpoises, puppies and panthers, to frogs, ferrets and fleas, no living creature was safe from Buckland's knife and fork. Guests at his dinner parties were often served up mice on toast – one of his favourite meals.

Bat out of hell

Once, when Buckland was visiting an Italian cathedral, a priest informed him that the slick floor was due to the miraculous blood of the sacrificed saints. Buckland promptly knelt down, ran his tongue across the floor and declared the liquid to be bat pee.

Keep it in the family

Buckland's son, **Francis**, shared his father's zoological culinary ambitions. Guests at Francis's home were served steaming boiled elephant trunk, fried porpoise heads, roasted giraffe necks and rhinoceros pie. Boa constrictor, sea slugs and earwigs were also eaten.

POO SWAPPING

The idea of taking poo from a healthy person and then putting it into another person might sound like the grossest thing you've ever heard. But it's real and it's called a **fecal transplant**. The procedure helps to restore the balance of bacteria in the gut of the person who receives the new poo and treat any gastrointestinal infections they have. Gross, but great!

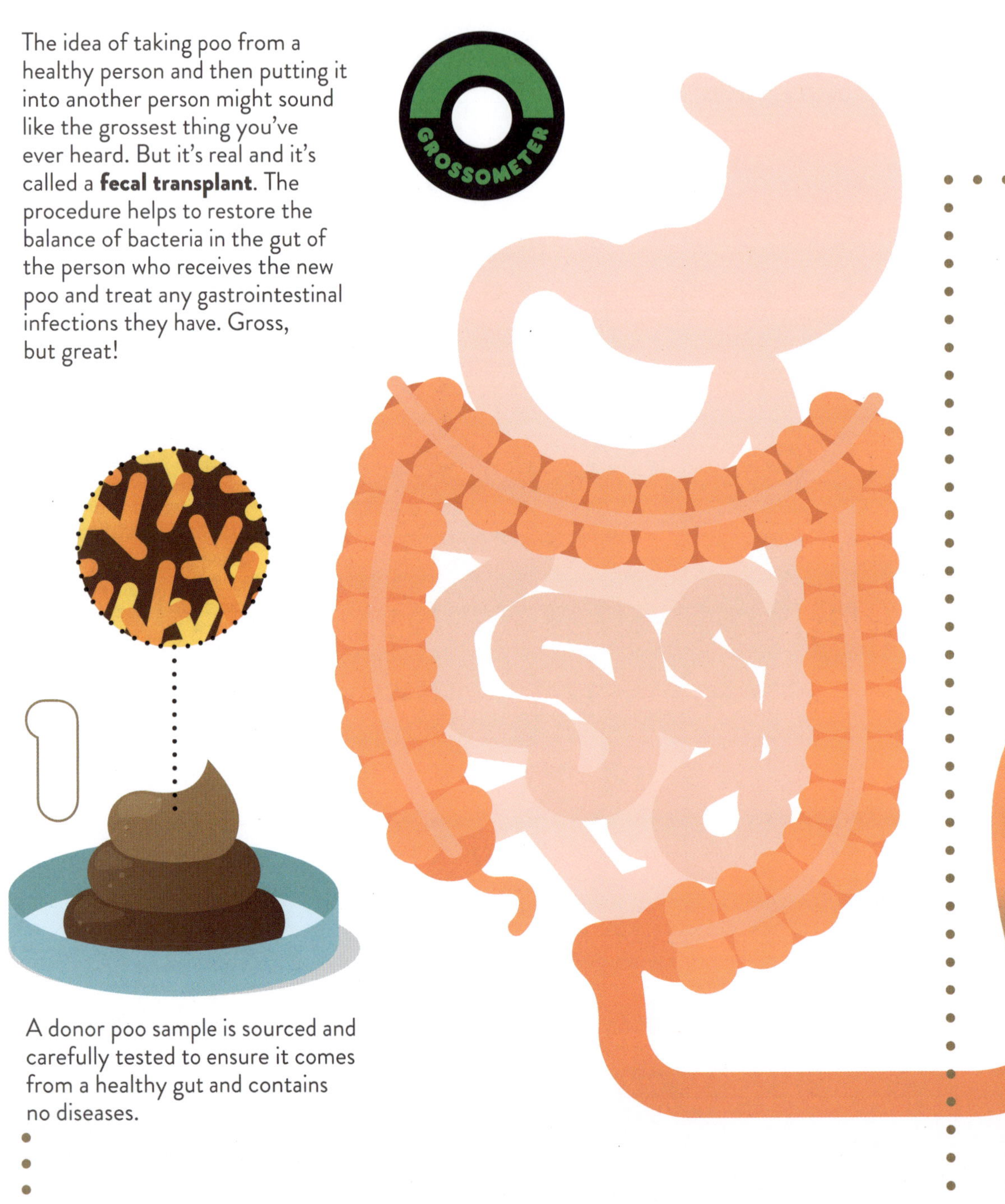

A donor poo sample is sourced and carefully tested to ensure it comes from a healthy gut and contains no diseases.

2

The poo sample is blended with a sterile saline solution to liquify it. This is then filtered to remove any large particles and frozen to allow storage.

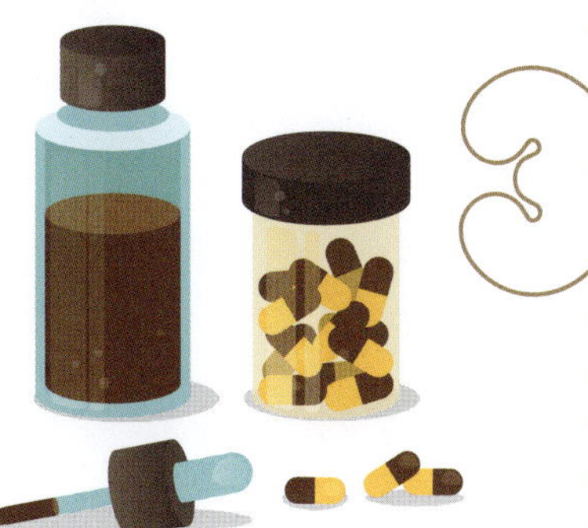

3

The poo sample is defrosted and then processed into a liquid or as capsules.

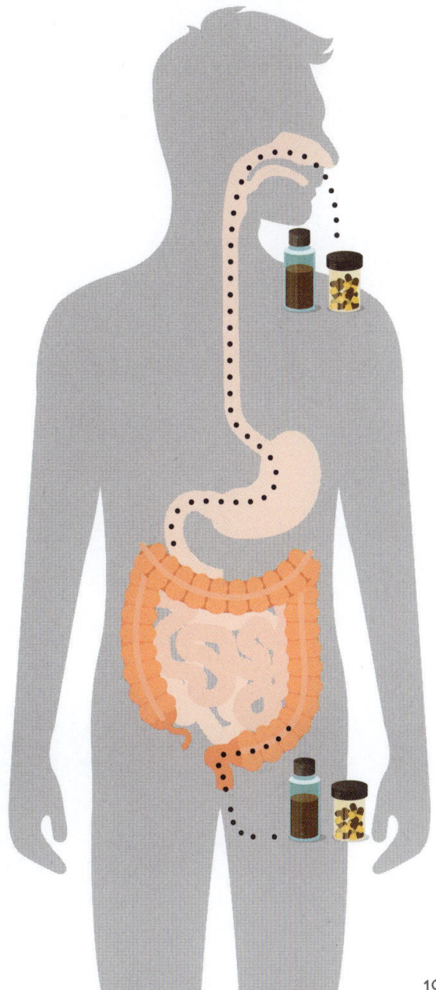

4

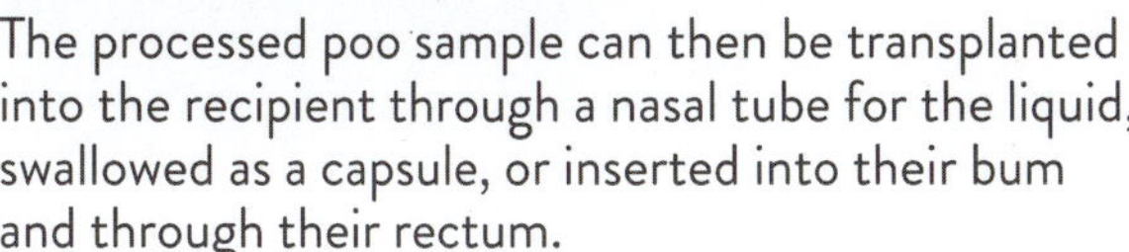

The processed poo sample can then be transplanted into the recipient through a nasal tube for the liquid, swallowed as a capsule, or inserted into their bum and through their rectum.

THE POO CHART

If you ever need to describe your poo, help is at hand. English doctors have devised the **Bristol Stool Chart** and according to them there are seven different types of poo – from tough little nuggets to liquid with no lumps at all.

Type 1

Separate, hard, nut-like lumps. If your poo looks like this, you are severely constipated and need to drink more water and add more fibre to your diet.

Type 2

A lumpy, sausage-shaped poo is an indication that you are mildly constipated.

Type 3

Sausage shaped, but with cracks on the surface. This is a healthy poo and an indication your digestive system is doing fine.

Type 4

A smooth, soft, snake-like poo is another healthy poo and again indicates all is healthy with your digestive system.

Type 5

Soft and blobby with clear-cut edges. It's very easy to pass and although it is a healthy poo, you may be lacking fibre in your diet.

Type 6

Mushy with fluffy pieces and ragged edges means you have mild diarrhea, and your body is battling illness by flushing toxins through your digestive tract. Can also be caused by infection, food intolerance or bowel disease.

Type 7

Entirely liquid with no solid pieces and indicates severe diarrhea. Again, your body is battling illness, infection, an intolerance or disease.

NIKOLA TESLA FELL IN LOVE WITH A PIGEON

Plenty of people like to feed the pigeons in the park, but Nikola Tesla didn't stop there. The famous scientist and inventor, best known for his pioneering research in electricity and robotics, used to find pigeons that were ill and take them back to his home. It was one of these rescued pigeons – a white dove – who stole his heart.

True love

In his own words, Tesla said: 'I loved that pigeon; I loved her as a man loves a woman and she loved me. When she was ill, I knew and understood; she came to my room and I stayed beside her for days. I nursed her back to health. That pigeon was the joy of my life. If she needed me, nothing else mattered. As long as I had her, there was a purpose in my life.'

Pigeons transmit diseases through their poo, which is infected with bacteria. Often the poo dries out on the street, windowsills and cars. It then becomes a powder, which is blown or kicked into the air and inhaled. Inhaling this poo powder is one way that the pathogens responsible for disease can be spread to humans.

Inconsolable

After the pigeon died, Tesla was said to have been inconsolable. Before the bird died, he claimed white light shone from her eyes, brighter than anything he had ever created with his electrical inventions. A heartbroken Tesla told his friends this was the moment he felt his life's work was finished.

MAGGOTS ARE USED IN MODERN MEDICINE

There are many kinds of therapies, such as aqua therapy, physical therapy and behavioral therapy, to help people recover from illness and injury. There is also a type of therapy that involves inserting live creepy, crawly and slimy little creatures into non-healing skin and soft-tissue wounds. **Maggot therapy** is amazing at cleaning out dead tissue in wounds and disinfecting them, because maggots love to eat dead tissue. They happily munch on rotting flesh, leaving healthy tissue virtually untouched. They even help the wound heal more quickly. Although maggot therapy has been around for thousands of years, its use in hospitals today requires conditions to be completely sterile.

The first step is to obtain flies whose larvae will only feed on dead, not live, tissue. The common green bottle fly is the most frequently used.

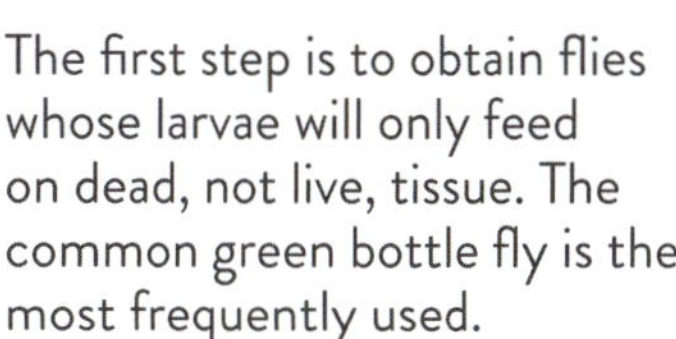

The flies lay their eggs and these are chemically sterilised using disinfectants.

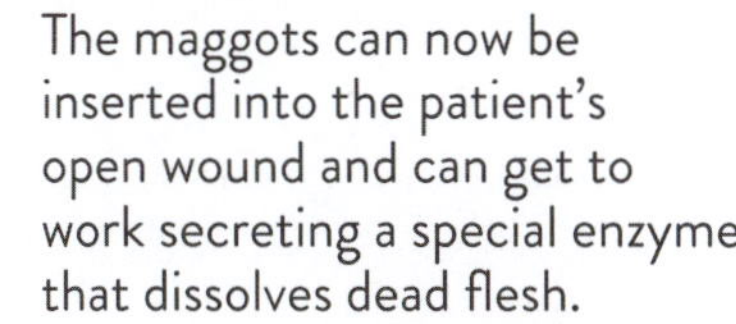

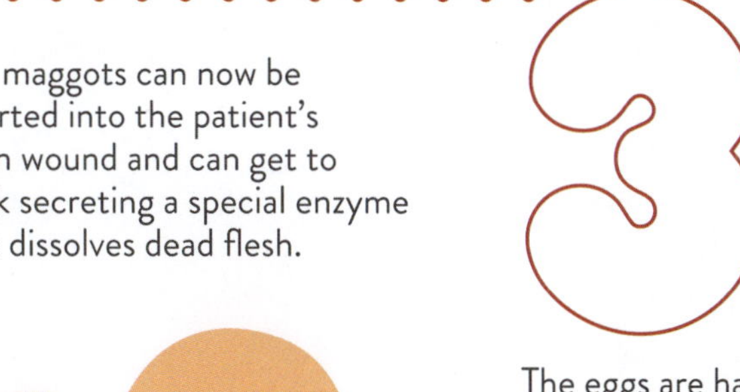

The maggots can now be inserted into the patient's open wound and can get to work secreting a special enzyme that dissolves dead flesh.

The eggs are hatched in sterilised conditions and the crawling larvae are ready for medical use.

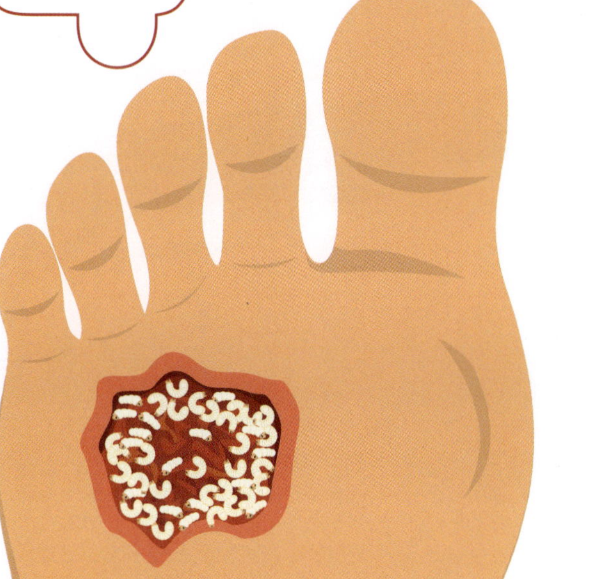

REVOLTING R

Humans love to create programmable machines to help make their lives a little easier: robots to do the vacuuming; robots to play their favourite music; robots to build cars. But there are some robots that are a bit more disgusting than a machine to mow your lawn.

Spew your guts

There's a robotic head whose sole purpose is to projectile vomit. He's called 'Larry' and he was built to study **norovirus**, an airborne illness that causes extreme stomach upsets. The regurgitating robot violently vomits, and the research team that built it tracks the spew particles to better understand how the virus travels.

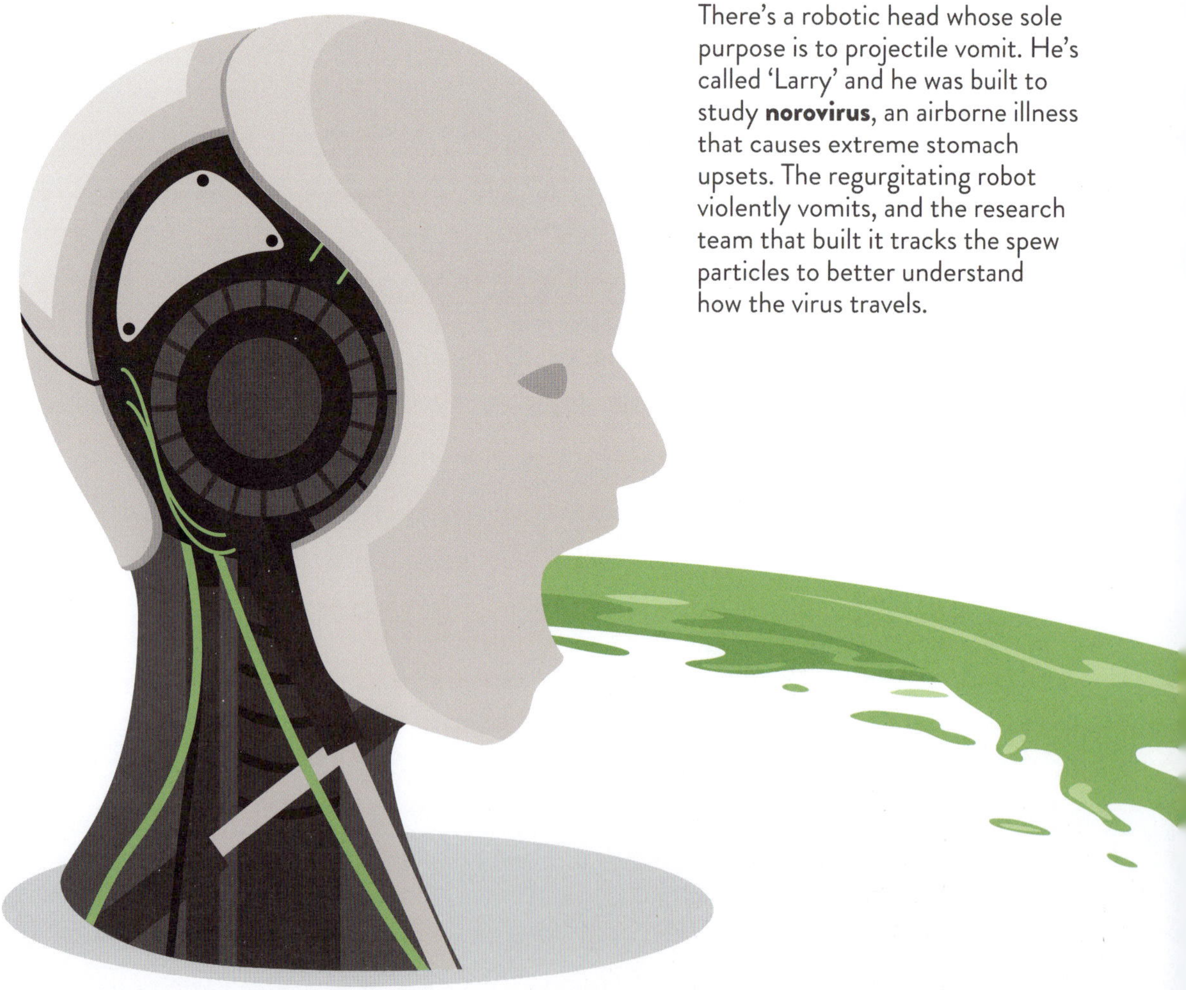

OBOTS

Passion pit

Robots are not usually recognised for their ability to perspire. Not the robotic armpit though, which emits Japanese industrial-recipe artificial sweat – a liquid that is usually used to test fabrics. The armpit even has curly hairs for extra grossness. The inventor of this robot believes that you only really empathise with someone when you smell and are revolted by their body odour.

Other revolting robots that have been created include a machine that can poo, a robot that mimics the symptoms of the disease swine flu, and a robotic bum.

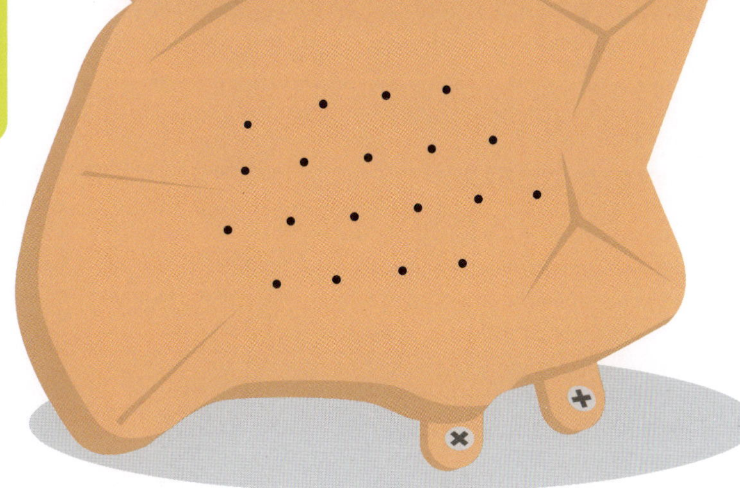

MUMMIES' BRAINS WERE REMOVED THROUGH THEIR NOSES WITH A HOOK

Ancient Egypt was the land of pharaohs, pyramids and treasure-filled tombs. It's also known for its methods of treating a dead body: an embalming process the ancient Egyptians called mummification. The process involved removing all the moisture from the body, which left a dried form that would not decay easily. All the internal organs that might decay rapidly were taken out first. This included the brain, which was removed by carefully putting special hooked instruments up through the nostrils so that the brain tissue could be mashed up into a goo and pulled out through the nose.

Have a heart

Once removed, the internal organs were preserved separately. The stomach, liver, lungs and intestines were all placed in special jars or boxes. The only organ left inside the body was the heart as they believed it to be the centre of a person's being and intelligence. The removed organs were then buried alongside the mummy.

Most people shaved their heads in ancient Egypt – not because this was the fashion but because there were **hair lice** everywhere! The tombs of Egyptian pharaohs were infested with the lice, which flooded from the remains of the bodies.

Drying out

The embalmers used natron, a type of salt, to remove all the moisture from the body. They would cover the body in it and even place additional packets inside the corpse where the organs had been removed. Once the body had dried out completely the embalmers would remove the packets.

MAKING A MUMMY

For the ancient Egyptians, making a mummy was a very long and painstaking process that could take months to complete. For you, though, there's a quicker way to see mummification in action. It still requires a bit of patience, but the results are absolutely worth it.

What you will need

Apple

Plastic zip lock bag

3 tablespoons table salt

3 tablespoons baking soda (sodium bicarbonate)

How to make a mummy

1. Take an apple and carefully carve a face into it.
2. Place the apple inside the plastic zip lock bag.
3. Mix the salt and baking soda together and add to the bag.
4. Shake the bag well until all moist areas are covered. Set aside in a cool dry place for **1 week**.
5. Remove the apple from the bag and carefully brush the salt and baking soda off it.
6. Remove excess salt and baking soda from the zip lock bag and place the apple back inside it. Set aside for a further **2 weeks**.
7. Remove the apple from the bag and dust off any salt and baking soda on the apple. If necessary give it a quick rinse.
8. Your apple has now been mummified!

The longer you leave the apple in the bag, the better your mummy will be.

BRAIN SURGERY IS PERFORMED WHILE THE PATIENT IS AWAKE

GROSSOMETER

The human brain has no pain receptors, which means that if someone could touch your brain you would be unaware of it. It's this lack of receptors that allows surgeons to sometimes operate on brains while the patient remains awake!

Know the drill

To gain access to the brain for the operation, surgeons shave some of the patient's hair and then remove part of the skull with a drill. Thankfully, the patients are sedated and sleepy during this part of the proceedings and also when the skull is reattached at the end of the surgery.

Question time

While operating on the brain, the surgeon may ask the fully awake patient questions or show them picture cards and monitor the activity in their brain as they respond. This helps the surgeon ensure that they are operating on the correct area and reduces the risk of damaging functional areas of the brain that control vision, movement or speech.

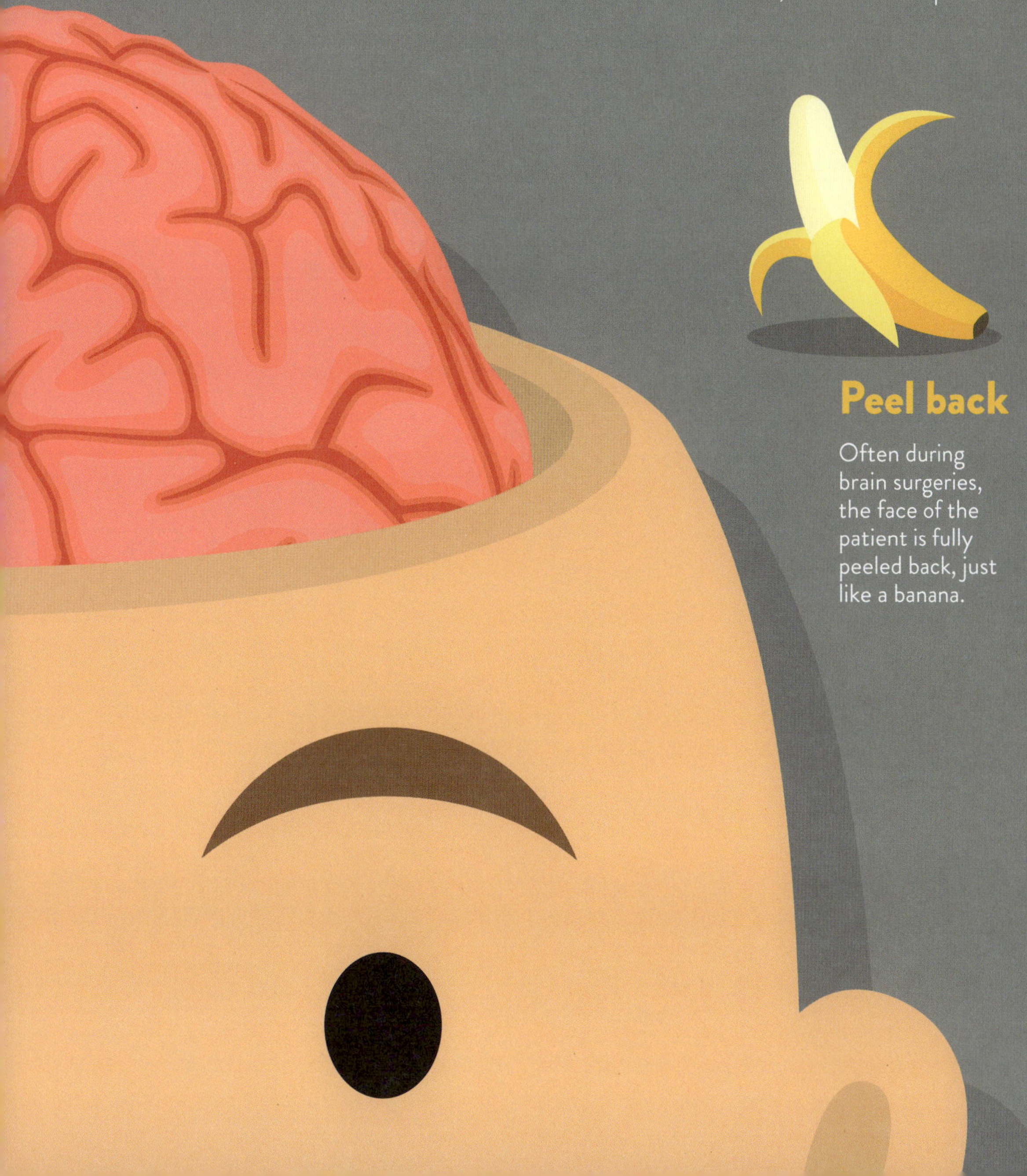

Peel back

Often during brain surgeries, the face of the patient is fully peeled back, just like a banana.

GROSS EXPLOSIONS

Explosions occur when a gas expands rapidly from a chemical reaction and releases an extreme amount of energy outwards. The results are very loud and very bright. But it's not just gunpowder and dynamite that create explosions – there are some gross ingredients too.

Bubbling mush

Some pig farms have exploded due to a highly explosive form of grey mushy foam that sometimes appears where large amounts of pig poo have collected. Among the gases in the bubbling foam are **methane** and **hydrogen sulphide**, both of which are highly flammable.

Beach blubber

When a whale dies, it usually sinks to the bottom of the ocean. But if the body of a dead whale inadvertently washes up on the shore there can be a buildup of gases inside it as it decomposes, resulting in an exploding whale and a beach covered in blubber.

Rotting whale carcasses have been exploded intentionally, using dynamite. The results have often been revolting as the blast has been too big, covering bystanders in blubber, blood and entrails as the whale burst into the sky.

Egg-splosion

Rotten eggs can explode. Bacteria inside the egg produce **hydrogen sulphide** and the resulting buildup of pressure eventually causes the egg to burst open and fling its stinky rotten insides sometimes up to **2 metres** in distance.

THE POWER OF POO AND PEE

The pee and poo that we dispose of down the toilet may be smelly and unappealing, but it can also be surprisingly beneficial, in a variety of ways. From powering buses to creating batteries, human waste is a versatile alternative fuel source.

PLOP 1

The poo bus

Buses normally run on diesel power, but not the UK's **Bio-Bus** which is powered by **biomethane,** a gas made from human poo and food waste. One tank of the gas will power the bus for **300 kilometres**. The bus even refuels at a local sewage works.

The pee battery

Microbial fuel cells can be powered by human pee. The benefit of using pee in this type of battery is that it's a free, readily available substance that can be used immediately.

The average healthy adult produces, on average, **34,400 litres** of pee in a lifetime. That's enough pee to fill over **230 bathtubs**.

This is the amount of poo a single adult produces every year.

SCIENTISTS PUT AN EAR ON A MOUSE

There are many icons of science, some of whom are featured in this book – famous physicists and mathematicians whose names are recognised the world over. However, there's one icon you may not have heard of: a little pink hairless mouse who had a human ear on its back. The **Vacanti mouse**, or '**Earmouse**', won't be appearing on any bank notes anytime soon, but the little rodent is most definitely a gross icon of science.

Dissolving

Over a few months, the mouse's blood vessels fed the cow cartilage cells that then grew into the biodegradable mould. Once the mould dissolved, the cartilage was able to support itself and the mouse now had an 'ear' on its back.

Mouldy

The 'ear' was actually an ear-shaped structure that was grown in a laboratory by putting cow cartilage cells into a biodegradable ear-shaped mould, which was then surgically implanted under the skin of the little mouse.

Immunity

The hairless mouse had virtually no immune system so its body did not reject the ear. The ear was never transplanted to a human because it was full of cow cells and would have been rejected by a human immune system.

Did you enjoy the book? Hopefully you found it extremely gross – some of those facts were really revolting. Which was your favourite? Did you discover the things you found the most disgusting using the grossometer? Were they the same as the things your friends and family found gross? But as well as being grim, gross, odious, offensive, horrid, horrible, rotten, revolting, despicable and downright disgusting, the facts were interesting too, right? That's the fabulous thing about reading a book like this: there's always something new to learn about the universe we live in, so keep your eyes and ears open. Especially for the gross stuff! When you do discover something new that makes you say 'Eww gross!' make sure you share it with someone else! Goodbye, for now.

About the author

Dan Marshall is a designer, illustrator and writer who has been drawing since he was a young child. It never fails to surprise him that as a grown-up he's now paid to do just that.

Along with *Eww Gross*, Dan has also published *Mind Blown*, *Look Book*, *No Way!* and *Super Duper*.

LOOK
BOOK
ABC for You and Me
Dan Marshall

NO WAY!
The Wildest Mind-Blowing Facts in the Universe
EARTH!
SCIENCE!
ANIMALS!
HUMANS!
MATHS!
Dan Marshall

MIND
BLOWN
DAN MARSHALL

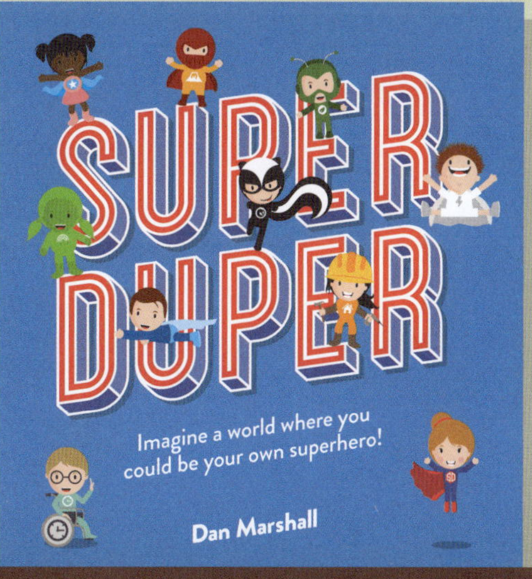
SUPER
DUPER
Imagine a world where you
could be your own superhero!
Dan Marshall